Exploring
Law and Culture

After awaiting trial for over 10 years, a Rwandan genocide suspect stands before his neighbors in a community court. The court was formed to speed up the prosecution of thousands of people accused of participating in the government-orchestrated slaughter of a half-million minority Tutsis and political moderates from the Hutu majority.

Exploring Law and Culture

Dorothy H. Bracey

John Jay College of Criminal Justice
and the Graduate School,
City University of New York

WAVELAND

PRESS, INC.

Long Grove, Illinois

For information about this book, contact:
  Waveland Press, Inc.
  4180 IL Route 83, Suite 101
  Long Grove, Illinois 60047-9580
  (847) 634-0081
  info@waveland.com
  www.waveland.com

Contents

Preface

Among anthropology's primary concerns are the maintenance of social order, the basis of political legitimacy, cultural change and cultural stability, and the ways in which culture is transmitted from one generation to the next. These concerns with social control have inevitably led to the study of law. This book is an introduction to the study of the relationship between law and culture. I hope it will appeal to students of anthropology, law and society, justice studies, and criminal justice.

Scholars of law and culture have used a multitude of approaches and topics. The ones represented here are primarily those that have proven most interesting to my students in courses such as Crime and Culture and Comparative Legal Systems. I have also tried to achieve a balance between the field's classics and studies that are more contemporary in either method or subject matter.

ACKNOWLEDGMENTS

I would like to thank the National Science Foundation for the Science Faculty Fellowship that allowed me to pursue the formal study of law at Yale Law School. The fact that Sally Falk Moore was Visiting Professor at the time made the experience especially valuable. Thanks are also due to the National Endowment for the Humanities for the Faculty Summer Seminar on Anthropology and Law at Princeton University; my research profited immeasurably from the assistance of the Princeton librarians, from the intellectual stimulation of my fellow seminarians, and particularly from the inspired leadership of Larry Rosen, whose contributions to the field place all of us in his debt. A PSC-CUNY grant supported fieldwork on the justice system of the People's Republic of China, while Australia's National Police Research Unit provided the opportunity for fieldwork among the Pitjinjara people of South Australia. I am deeply grateful to the faculty and staff of John Jay College's Lloyd George Sealy Library as well as to my colleagues in the Department of Anthropology. I would also like to acknowledge my debt to the late June Starr, whose collegiality and companionship are sorely missed.

Serena Nanda and Deborah Reed-Danahay provided extremely thoughtful and useful reviews of the manuscript. Very special thanks are due to Waveland Press and Tom Curtin for constant encouragement and incredible patience. Both the style and the accuracy of this text owe much to Jeni Ogilvie. To Tom Johnson, who provided the perfect combination of unceasing support and gentle nagging, gratitude from the bottom of my heart.

Chapter One

Law's Cultural Context

Imagine a freshman or sophomore college student somewhere in New York state who's going out to buy what David Letterman might call a "refreshing alcoholic beverage." Perhaps she's thinking of going to the grocery store to pick up a six-pack of Miller Lite. Has she celebrated her 21st birthday? No? Sorry this is New York, where the law forbids anyone under 21 from buying any alcoholic beverage.

Ah, but you say the young woman is 21 and she is planning a romantic dinner with her boyfriend. Then perhaps a medium-priced bottle of wine is in order. Sorry, she won't find that "alcoholic beverage" in a grocery store; in New York wines and hard liquor can be sold only in a special store licensed by the state. And those stores must be closed on Sunday mornings. Should she and her boyfriend decide to have a restaurant brunch on Sunday with a glass of fresh orange juice sparkled up with a bit of Champagne, sorry, no liquor will be sold before noon.

What if the young woman has a cousin living in Canada? Her cousin could buy any "alcoholic beverage" after he turned 19—except in the provinces of Alberta, Manitoba, and Quebec where the minimum purchase age is 18; in Manitoba and New Brunswick, those under 18 may not purchase liquor but they may consume it in bars under adult supervision. Across the Atlantic in Denmark, on the other hand, 16-year-olds may buy alcohol, but they may not consume it in public until they are 18. In some cantons (counties), the Swiss may buy beer and wine when they turn 14. Azerbaijan, Nigeria, Jamaica, and China allow the purchase of alcohol at any age.

1

Yet, in Saudi Arabia and in the Navajo Nation in America's Southwest, it is not legal to purchase liquor regardless of age. The United States raised the minimum age to 21 in 1987, New Zealand lowered it to 18 in 2000, and the Netherlands considered raising the legal age but decided to leave it unchanged. Malaysia, South Korea, and Ukraine are the only nations besides the United States to set the minimum legal drinking age at 21.

What's going on here? Are these differences in law just random events? Possibly. But it is also possible—and more likely—that the different laws reflect different cultural assumptions about the transition from childhood to adulthood. They may indicate different values concerning individual responsibility or altered states of consciousness. They may mirror perceptions of alcohol consumption as a sin, as a necessary evil, or as a positive good. They may be a product of particular historical experiences. Or they may be the result of lobbying by certain groups, such as liquor dealers or religious organizations, who have the ability and opportunity to influence the legislative process to attain benefits related to their interests. Looking at the relationships among law, assumptions, values, and the allocation of power is looking at law in its *cultural context*.

CULTURE

Culture is often defined as shared assumptions, values, interests, and the behavior based upon them. Assumptions are facts or statements that are taken for granted, that do not require proof. Some groups assume that the transition from childhood to adulthood comes early and easily; others assume that it comes late and is accompanied by rebellion and defiance. Some assume that drinks such as wine and beer are foods, beneficial when consumed in moderate amounts; others assume that all alcoholic beverages are harmful and ideally to be avoided. We would expect to find these differing assumptions to be reflected in differing laws.

Values refer to things that are prized and sought after or disdained and avoided. Words such as "good" and "bad" are often associated with values. Some cultural groups value rationality and self-control; they often perceive alcohol as a threat to these qualities. Others may value conviviality, while still others value occasions on which inhibitions are dropped and the mind reaches beyond its ordinary state. Again, we would expect that these cultural groups would differ in respect to their laws about alcohol.

Interests are related to values but are by no means identical. If values can be expressed in terms of a general sense of "good" or "bad," interests are expressed in terms of "good or bad for me." Even people who share values and assumptions may find that they have different interests. Producers of alcoholic beverages share many assumptions and values with liquor store owners and may even have many interests in common with them, but the two groups also have interests that diverge. For example, vintners, brewers, and distillers want to make it easy for buyers to purchase their products and therefore support laws that allow supermarkets to sell alcoholic beverages. Owners of liquor stores fear that they cannot compete with supermarkets on issues such as price and hours of operation, so they support laws that limit venues for alcohol sale.

Differences in assumptions, values, and interests lead to differences in behavior. People who believe that becoming an adult is a gradual learning process, who see alcohol as a food, and who value the ability to relax in the company of others probably tend to consume alcohol with meals, do most of their drinking at home or restaurants, and do so in the company of family and friends. Those who see adulthood and self-control as attributes that come only after several decades of life may view alcohol as a privilege of adulthood and thus drink away from home and in the company of peers. People who see maturation as a time of conflict and see alcohol as a threat to self-control may abstain from alcohol use. Accommodating such different behaviors requires different laws.

It is rare that all members of a group—even a small group—share all the same values and assumptions. People who work long hours for low wages may value the escape that liquor can provide. Their employers may value the punctuality and alertness that result from sobriety. Young people who see drinking as a sign of adulthood may have parents who see it as a danger their children are not ready to handle. Religious groups that consider alcoholic beverages as a natural result of fermenting grapes or grains—and therefore part of Creation's bounty—may coexist with religious groups that consider such beverages the work of the devil. The question of whose assumptions, values, and behaviors become enshrined in law is a question of the distribution of power and the workings of the legal process.

THEORIES OF LAW

Although there are many ways in which values are translated into laws, they tend to fall into one of three broad categories (Akers 1997:137–158). The first is through *consensus*, which means that the law reflects the values of the vast majority of the population. For example, most contemporary Westerners believe that entering a stranger's home and taking something without the owner's permission is a bad thing and should be punished. Even most burglars probably subscribe to that opinion—either they hope not to be caught or else they try to show that their actions do not actually constitute burglary. They rarely try to defend themselves by saying that burglary is actually a good thing.

Second, laws can be the result of *conflict* between or among different groups within a culture. In this case, one group wishes to impose its values and assumptions upon others or to see its interests furthered at the expense of others. In this situation we see the workings of political power. Although the criminologist George Vold was addressing primarily industrialized societies, his observations have broader application:

> The whole political process of law making, law breaking, and law enforcement becomes a direct reflection of deep-seated and fundamental conflicts between interest groups and their more general struggles for the control of the police power of the state. Those who produce legislative majorities win control over the police power and dominate the policies that decide who is likely to be involved in violation of the law. (Vold 1958:208–209)

The legal results of conflict can be seen most clearly in colonial societies or in other situations in which one country has conquered another one. The victorious nation is obviously in a position to promulgate laws furthering its own values and interests. This is also true in hereditary aristocracies, societies with major discrepancies in wealth, and in societies that contain one or more minority groups. In some societies, religious specialists, men, or elders control the law-making power.

The third category is *compromise*. Pluralistic conflict or interest group processes involve a number of groups, no one of which can maintain power over a period of time. These social, religious, political, economic, hereditary, or occupational elites have some assumptions, values, and interests in common but they differ on others. They form alliances, negotiate, bargain, and compromise.

Having laid out all these factors that go into the making of law, it is important to point out that none of them is static. Assumptions yield to new information; values are transformed as access to resources changes or as friends and peer groups shift; interests vary from time to time. Alliances shift. Outside forces intervene. People who once wielded power find themselves subject to the power of others. In even the most traditional of societies, culture is constantly changing and law changes with it. And so it's possible that the young lady setting out to buy a bottle of wine in New York may, someday, pick it up at a grocery store just as she could do in California or New Mexico.

LAW AND OTHER NORMS

Of course, law is not the only thing that affects drinking behavior. To begin with, some people simply disobey the law, purchasing alcohol at an illegal age or from unauthorized sources. But the law is usually silent on whether one should drink grape wine or palm wine, bourbon, ouzo, sake, aguardiente, rum, tequila, or gin. It rarely has anything to do with whether people binge in the company of their friends or sip around the family dining table. It does not usually indicate whether women's drinking patterns should differ from those of men or whether the middle-aged should drink in the same manner as the elderly. Law joins with norms, mores, custom, fashion, and even fad to create the entire repertoire of drinking rules. This repertoire is often referred to as *social control*.

If this is true of drinking behavior, it is also true of most other types of behavior. It therefore becomes necessary to distinguish legal rules from all other types of rules, and thus we are confronted with the sticky task of defining "law."

"Those of us who have learned humility have given over the attempt to define law" (Radin 1938:1151). Anthropologists and other social scientists who have tried to develop a cross-cultural definition of law—a definition that will be useful regardless of the culture being studied—sympathize with Radin. Nevertheless, when these social scientists engage in discussions of law, they need something that will ensure that they are discussing the same thing.

In the early 1950s, E. Adamson Hoebel (1954) identified two related problems that continue to bedevil cross-cultural legal studies. One is excessive parochialism and the other is the fact that law is only one part of the web of social control with no clear edges to separate it from the rest (18). Parochialism is the tendency to rigidly use one's own terms, concepts, and institutions when examining other cultures. In trying to distinguish law from other forms of social control, it is tempting for Westerners to look for legislatures, police officers, and courts and, if these cannot be found, to declare that the group in question does not have law, only custom. The opposite tendency—displayed by some early anthropologists—is to declare that law is any sort of rule that regulates social behavior, and therefore all social control is law. Neither of these extreme formulations is satisfactory.

Many students of law have looked to the school of jurisprudence known as legal realism for an answer. Legal realists look to how law actually works (law in action) rather than to what the rules may say (law on the books). Justice Benjamin Cardozo presented the classic statement of legal realism when he defined law as "a principle or rule of conduct so established as to justify a prediction with reasonable certainty that it will be enforced by the courts if its authority is challenged" (1924:52). Cardozo is suggesting that three elements comprise the definition of law: (1) rules; (2) a mechanism for applying the rules to specific instances; and (3) a mechanism for enforcing the rules.

Taking Cardozo's approach a step further, many social scientists totally abandoned the search for a definition of law and instead looked for attributes of law. One advantage of this method is that it does not force a dichotomy between law on the one hand and all other forms of social control on the other. Since a rule may have some but not all the attributes of law, it is possible to conceptualize a continuum of rules that control social behavior.

Leopold Pospisil (1978) developed one of the earliest and most influential sets of attributes of law. He began by deciding that law consisted of principles abstracted from decisions, but that not all such principles were law. Using his knowledge of a broad range of cultures, he isolated four criteria that appeared to identify legal rules.

1. *Authority.* Pospisil identifies authority as an individual or group whose decisions are followed by a majority of the group's

members. Individuals either accept the authority's decisions or have acceptance forced upon them. He suggests that it is this attribute of authority that distinguishes custom from law (30–43).

2. ***Intention of Universal Application.*** Pospisil distinguishes legal from political judgments by attributing to the former the intention that the judgment be applied to all similar cases in the future. An explicit declaration of this intention may be made while pronouncing the judgment; a reference may be made to a precedent or established custom or rule; it may be tacitly assumed; or it may be implicit in the form or grammatical construct used by the adjudicator (43–46).

3. ***Obligatio.*** Pospisil borrows this term from Roman law, where it applies to the contract or relationship between litigants. He uses it in this context to refer to the "socio-legal relationship of the two litigants as it supposedly existed at the time of the violation of the law, together with the delict (illegal act) which unbalanced the relationship" (46). It is a description of the rights and duties of the parties and of the loss suffered because one of the parties failed in his duties (46–48).

4. ***Sanction.*** Although some authors have equated law with the presence of sanction, Pospisil points out that some nonlegal decisions carry sanctions also. He emphasizes the fact that not all sanctions are physical punishment; fines, ridicule, ostracism, avoidance, and reprimands also serve as sanctions in many cultures. He defines legal sanction as "either a negative device— withdrawing rewards or favors that would have been granted if the law had not been violated—or as a positive measure for inflicting some painful experience, physical or psychological" (51).

Depending on attributes rather than definitions helps to avoid the problems identified by Hoebel—the danger of parochialism and isolating law from other forms of social control. Looking for and at attributes allows anthropologists and other social scientists to look at law as only one of a number of enforceable norms and to examine "law-like" activities, both formal and informal, and at levels reaching from the international to the extremely local (Moore 2005:1).

THIS BOOK

This book's underlying premise is that the relationship between law and culture is a two-way relationship. This means that not only does culture provide a tool for the study of law, but also that law provides a tool for the study of culture. To illustrate this I rely heavily upon my own discipline of anthropology but also draw concepts, ideas, and example from sociology, criminology, political science, history, the law and society movement, and several approaches developed by lawyers, e.g. legal realism. Each chapter of this book will examine a different aspect of the relationship between law and culture.

The following chapter deals with the history of studies of law and culture. This reveals that many of the issues that intrigued early students about the relationship between law and culture are still the focus of studies today. This chapter also looks at method—at what members of various disciplines actually do when they are studying law and culture.

Chapter 3 begins the study of different families of laws and the cultures in which they are found. It gives the rationale for using a three-part typology and provides a brief description of each family of law. The chapter warns that even in a scheme with only three categories, the lines between categories are often blurred. It also introduces the concept of legal pluralism. This is the recognition of the fact that different systems of law may coexist within national boundaries and that national systems of law must coexist with various forms of international law.

Chapter 4 concerns the law that arose in Western Europe and England and that also exists today in the countries that were once European colonies. Since this is the law and the culture that are most familiar to the majority of readers of this book, it provides a natural starting place.

Chapter 5 deals with religious law, primarily Islamic and Jewish law. It examines the origins of these religious systems as well as the cultural and historic circumstances surrounding their birth. It goes on to show how differently Islamic and Jewish law are applied in different countries.

Chapter 6 is about customary or traditional law. Although all legal systems rely on tradition to some extent, the systems considered here look primarily to custom and tradition for guidance. Of particular note is that such systems are not frozen in the past but have mechanisms that allow them to adapt to changing conditions. In fact, traditional legal systems today provide inspiration for other systems that once considered them primitive and doomed to disappear.

Chapter 7 looks at some of the ways in which anthropologists have studied the U.S. legal system. It dwells on those parts of the legal process that take place outside of the courtroom, such as preliminary hearings and plea bargaining. It shows that plaintiffs and defendants as well as police officers and court clerks can be as important as judges and legislators in determining exactly what the law will be.

Chapter 8 follows chapter 7 by looking at laws deliberately and consciously designed by one group to change the behavior of another; examples include the outlawing of the Northwest Coast potlatch and the suttee of India. Specifically, this chapter examines the colonialist use of law to destroy the culture of the colonized. It demonstrates how law can be used as a tool of acculturation and domination.

The final chapter looks at the implications of having one legal system in a culturally pluralistic nation and at the attempts to raise a "cultural defense." Examples include the effects of Norwegian divorce law on Muslim immigrants, the Amish objection to compulsory education, and the sacramental use of peyote by the Native American Church.

DOING COMPARATIVE STUDIES

Comparative studies usually begin with a series of descriptions; often, this is also where they end. But comparative studies are most valuable—and also most interesting—when they are used to answer questions. The nature of the questions, of course, depends on the interests of the student. What follows are suggested questions that begin with broad concepts and build from there (Barton et al. 1983:373–375).

    1. What is the perceived function of the legal system? Is it retribution, the punishment of those who have defied the rules? Is it deterrence, to set an example to warn others not to misbehave, and thereby to reinforce the community's norms? Is it rehabilitation, to return the transgressor back

into a law-abiding member of the group? Or is it restoration—to return the situation to what it was before the law was broken or the dispute arose? Are the functions different at different times? Are they the same for all members of the group? Is there an attempt to combine more than one function? Is the attempt successful?

2. Are people seen as correctable or not? Does the possibility of rehabilitation appear to apply equally to all people, regardless of gender, class, or ethnic group? Does it appear to vary with age; for example, are young people perceived as being easier to correct than old people. Are these perceptions explicit, that is, do people acknowledge them openly? Are the perceptions consistent with the practice?

3. What is most import and most in need of protection—the rights of the individual or the rights of the group? Are the rights of all individuals protected equally? If not, who gets more or less protection? Which group's rights are most important—nuclear family, kinship group such as clan or lineage, or political group such as tribe, community, or nation?

4. Does the group see itself as being largely law abiding, with a small number of deviant acts committed by a small number of people? Or is deviance perceived as a major threat to the well-being of the community?

5. What is most easily and/or most often harmed by deviance? Human life and safety? Property? Privilege? The relationship between the human and the supernatural?

6. Who are the actors in the legal system? Are they full-time specialists? Do they have special training? Or is their status in the legal system a result of their status in the political, religious, or kinship systems? Does the legal system consist of many different roles or is the cast rather small? What—if any—part is played by friends, relatives, or the general public?

7. Is access to the legal system easy or difficult? Do plaintiffs have to wait a long time to have their cases heard? Are there fees or other obstacles? Is access the same for all or does it vary with age, gender, wealth, or other variables?

8. At what point in the dispute or deviance does the legal system intervene? Does it make itself felt at the first sign of

deviance, on the assumption that small digressions, if uncorrected, inevitably lead to large ones? Or does the culture respect the right of individuals to exhibit a broad variety of behavior, invoking the legal system only when major problems arise and then responding with major sanctions?

9. Does the culture regard all persons as being equal before the law or does it make distinctions of status, gender, age, or ethnicity? Are the distinctions explicit or are they seen only in practice? Are elite individuals held to higher or lower standards? Are their punishments heavier or lighter?

10. Who brings a complaint? Is it left to a dissatisfied party or someone who feels victimized? Are the complainants' statuses specialized such as police or prosecutors? How much discretion do they have? Can any member of the community call attention to a dispute or a wrong?

11. What kinds of evidence are accepted? Is physical or eyewitness evidence given special weight? Does the reputation of the disputants or the accused play any part? What qualifies a witness? Is there cross-examination? What is the role of the supernatural—are there omens or ordeals? Is a confession considered necessary—or even desirable? Does evidence of contrition affect the severity of punishment?

12. What penalties are available? Does the system provide for restitution or compensation in the form of money, goods, or labor? Are there fines and, if so, what happens to the money or goods so collected? Is there a death penalty, banishment, or corporal punishment in the form of whipping, branding, or amputation? Are there facilities for imprisonment or forced labor? Do sanctions take the form of loss of status or privilege?

13. How effective is the system? What is the rate of recidivism? Are people generally satisfied with the outcome or do they see the legal system as ineffective, biased, or corrupt?

Chapter Two

History and Method

Law fascinated early anthropologists. Law is, after all, one of the ways in which human beings regulate the relationship between individuals and the group, the obligations of kinship, the issues of descent and property, the handling of disputes, the rules of status and power, and the distinction between the sacred and the secular. It is a tool for maintaining the status quo and it is an implement of change. No wonder that the study of culture and the study of law often are closely intertwined. The issues of theory and method faced by the early legal anthropologists are quite similar to the issues faced by their descendants today.

EARLY ANTHROPOLOGY AND LAW

Several of anthropology's founders had legal training; they turned to anthropology in hopes of finding answers posed by their studies of law. New Yorker Lewis Henry Morgan (1818–1881), referred to by some as the "father of American anthropology" (Cole 1977:350), provides a prominent example. His legal background led to his interest in the rules of descent, inheritance, kinship, and political organization among his Iroquois neighbors, an interest that inspired his most famous work, *Ancient Society* (1877), an attempt to formulate an evolutionary theory of human society. Morgan was strongly influenced by nineteenth-century concepts of progress. He hypothesized a process by which all human cultures moved from savagery through barbarism and finally achieved civilization. Morgan's work on Iroquois law and kinship is still cited. His evolutionary theory, however, has been discredited for ignoring the fact that societies actually do not follow his three-stage pattern and instead develop in many different ways. Nor did he recognize the fact that cultures often borrow from each other.

Morgan's English contemporary, Cambridge law professor Sir Henry James Sumner Maine (1822–1888), was also influenced by theories of evolution and progress. He began his study of Roman law hoping a historical and comparative view would improve his understanding of British law. He was struck by the fact that Roman law—particularly property law—recognized the family as being far more important than the individual. From this observation, Maine developed a grand scheme to describe the progress of law and government from the group-centeredness of the earliest humans to the splendid individualism of his own time. Maine's most enduring contribution to legal anthropology is his understanding of the relationship between legal and cultural change. The prime example is his distinction between kin-based societies in which rights and duties are based solely on the family relationships and social *status* of the people involved and other societies in which individuals *contract* voluntarily with other individuals. Maine's evolutionary perspective led him to theorize that the former came earlier and in time gave way to the latter.

Morgan spent much time with the Iroquois and Maine had served as a civil servant in India, with his duties often taking him into villages. Nevertheless, both men based much of their work on library research, rather than on fieldwork and firsthand observation.

THE INTRODUCTION OF FIELDWORK

Legal anthropology changed dramatically in the 1920s and '30s with the work of Bronislaw Malinowski. Malinowski spent years on the Trobriand Islands near New Guinea and wrote about almost every aspect of Melanesian culture. He did not try to account for all cultures and all times, but confined himself to Melanesia and wrote only what he learned from his own fieldwork. Since he was not a lawyer, Malinowski did not identify law mainly with legal institutions but instead with all aspects of social control. He pointed out that the Trobrianders had no police, legislators, or courts, but they did have rules. He showed that the group enforced those rules and controlled its members with gossip, insult, ridicule, and contempt, devices that could lead offenders to reform their behavior, remove themselves from the group, or in extreme cases, attempt or commit suicide. Maine had postulated that in early stages of social evolution, "the individual was so much submerged in the group that, as an individual, he could not commit a crime or be punished for it" (Orenstein 1968:265). By showing that the rules and punishments of the Trobrianders did indeed apply to individuals and not to kin groups, Malinowski did much to undermine evolutionary theories of law. Later fieldworkers such as Robert Redfield and Leopold Pospisil challenged other aspects of Maine's evolutionary theories, showing that all societies have both status and contract, although they usually emphasize one or the other (Rouland 2005:23).

One of Malinowski's greatest contributions to the study of law was to show that it could be studied using the ethnographic method. He lived among the Trobrianders for four years, rigorously avoiding the company of Europeans and participating as fully as possible in the daily lives of the villagers. He communicated only in the native language and took copious notes. He slowly formulated theories and then tested them against what he saw and heard. Although legal anthropologists have added other methods to their repertoire, ethnography is still the foundation upon which other techniques are built. By turning away from the study of legal institutions and concentrating instead on the behavior associated with disputes and social control, Malinowski helped to shift legal anthropology from being a subdiscipline of jurisprudence to its current status as a social and behavioral science.

Malinowski saw traditional societies as being stable and self-contained, composed of interrelated parts that maintained equilibrium. He wanted to know how that equilibrium was maintained. How did societies get their members to conform to the rules and how did they sanction those who did not? How did they deal with disputes and hostilities within the group? Attempts to answer this question preoccupied many British social anthropologists, particularly those who worked in British colonial Africa, including such well-known people as Meyer Fortes, S. F. Nadel, and E. E. Evans-Pritchard.[1]

LAW AS PROCESS

Other anthropologists of law conceived of societies as open systems; that is, they affected and were affected by their political and economic environments. In addition, even small societies might contain groups whose interests were in conflict. Thus, it was impossible to take the rules as a starting point; instead, it was necessary to ask who made the rules, who changed them, who applied them, and to whom they were applied and under what circumstances. This school of anthropologists gradually became less interested in the rules themselves and more interested in the processes by which disputes were settled, conflict was handled, and change was accommodated. It comes as no great surprise to learn that the former approach came to be known as rule-centered and the latter as processual. Names associated with the processual approach include Max Gluckman, P. H. Gulliver, and Victor Turner.[2]

No one did more to define law as process rather than as rules and outcomes than Laura Nader. This interest was reflected in the title of the influential book (1978) she produced together with several of her students—*The Disputing Process: Law in Ten Societies.* Each of the contributors studied dispute settlement in a different culture, tracing "developments and shifts in the balance of power between the individuals involved . . . to focus on the strategies used by litigants in obtaining a desired end" (8). From these, Nader identified seven procedural modes used in attempts to deal with grievances, conflicts, and disputes: (1) "lumping it" or failing to press a complaint; (2) avoidance, or withdrawing from a disputed situation; (3) coercion, in which one forces an outcome on another; (4) negotiation, in which the two principle parties work out a solution without a third party; (5) mediation, in which a third party helps the disputants work out a solution; (6) arbitration, with the parties agreeing to accept beforehand the judgment of a mutually acceptable third party; and (7) adjudication, where a third party has the authority to render and enforce a decision whether or not it is acceptable to each or any of the parties involved (10–11).

PIGEONS AND PARAKEETS

A different type of disagreement about the proper approach to law arose in 1965, when Max Gluckman took issue with Paul Bohannan's method in his *Justice and Judgment Among the Tiv*. Bohannan had asserted that the Western legal vocabulary (and the concepts underlying it) was a Western "folk system" and that to apply such a system to a description of the Tiv of Nigeria was illegitimate. Instead, Bohannan insisted that the anthropologist's job is to describe the legal system as the people themselves—in this case, the Tiv—see it. He emphasized that anthropology is about context and he suggested that to fit Tiv data into a model of Western jurisprudence was similar to "squeezing parakeets into pigeonholes" (1989:vii).

Gluckman believed that anthropologists who confine themselves to reporting the way in which a society sees itself are falling into the trap of solipsism, a theory that says we can know nothing outside of ourselves. Gluckman argued that Bohannan's approach meant we could know only the Tiv (or any other society) and could not progress to a wider understanding of the ways in which human beings maintained social order. He advocated a comparative method, one in which societies could be compared across a number of variables. Although Bohannan was not comfortable with the concepts, it is possible to see the Bohannan/Gluckman controversy as an example of the *emic-etic* formula. Using terms borrowed from linguistics, some anthropologists have advocated an emic approach in which the anthropologist tries to convey to the reader the way in which the studied culture views itself—to enable the reader to see the world and the culture through the eyes of a member of that culture. This approach values depth and context, but tends to view the studied culture in isolation. The etic approach, on the other hand, is deliberately comparative; it looks for variables that can be studied across cultures and hopes to find generalizations. It is probably safe to say that the majority of contemporary legal anthropologists favor the Bohannan view; nevertheless, comparisons—especially comparisons with the researcher's own culture—are never very far from the surface.

LAW AND POWER

Another concern of many contemporary legal anthropologists is the relation of law to social structure, economics, and power. This interest is closely related to the works of Laura Nader and June Starr (Nader and Todd 2002; Starr and Collier 1989). These scholars are less interested in the content of the rules and processes than in the ways in which law does or does not mirror the existing power structure. They are also alert to instances in which law can be used to subvert the existing power structure and to the ways in which people resist laws that they consider unfair. Studies such as these make us aware of the effects of colonialism and national governments; of multinational corporations and financial institutions such as the World Bank; of the status of women, children, and minorities; and of the social, economic, and political differences that may exist within the group and that may be subject to change.

The emphasis on power and process has provided a valuable corrective framework and complement to the earlier emphasis on rules and institutions. To some observers, however, it portrays societies as being made up exclusively of individuals busily manipulating the system for their own ends and acting in a moral vacuum. Comaroff and Roberts (1981) presented a picture of Tswana (of Botswana) disputing grounded in Tswana ideology, assumptions, and values. For Comaroff and Roberts and their adherents, parties to disputes act not only to maximize their own material interests, but also do so in the context of their culture's values and beliefs. Disputants try to bring about certain outcomes, but they also want to be vindicated—to be seen as upholding the norms they share with other members of their group. They want to be seen—and to see themselves—as good people. Therefore they invoke not only their culture's rules and processes but also the moral foundations on which those rules and processes are based. The fact that opposing parties can each find moral bases for their actions reflects society's complexity. One of the tasks of the scholar is to explain how third parties and observers interpret the validity and moral claims of the disputants.

A model study of this type is Rosen's (1989) analysis of the court of Sefrou, Morocco. He finds that the *qadi*, the judge, of the court is not particularly concerned with precedent or consistency in his decisions, "but rather in the fit between the decisions of the Muslim judge and the cultural concepts and social relations to which they are inextricably tied" (18). Neither the qadi nor the people who attend his court are particularly interested in building up a logically coherent body of law; instead, they expect decisions that cohere to the expectations, beliefs, and values of the entire culture as it currently exists, coherence to all those things that give life meaning. Both judge and people of Sefrou, for example, share the belief that people will continue to act in the same ways in which they have habitually acted, and in ways in which their backgrounds, characters, and personalities suggest they will do. Therefore, records of past convictions, information about a person's family and origins, and the testimonials of neighbors and associates are important evidence. Rosen's work is an example of the type of study that tries to understand law by analyzing the meanings and interpretations that people give to different aspects of the disputing process.

THE QUESTION OF METHOD

The questions that scholars ask, the assumptions they make, and the hypotheses they test influence the methods they use. When Llewellyn and Hoebel (1941) wanted to learn about the "law-ways" of the Cheyenne people in North America as they had existed half a century earlier, they could not observe Cheyenne legal behavior nor could they consult written records. What they could do was interview a group of Cheyenne elders with good memories. Llewellyn and Hoebel asked these older Cheyenne to tell them about deviance and disputes from the past and how such incidences were handled. They were interested in "cases of hitch or trouble," cases in which people did not behave as the culture's norms would have dictated. They asked the elders to give them examples of such instances and to explain what happened afterwards. When the informants finished their stories, Llewellyn and Hoebel would ask questions, some designed to elicit further facts (names, dates, places, relationships), others more concerned with the attitudes of the speakers and their perception of the attitudes of others. Further questions dealt with motivations ("Why did he do that?") and evoked "felt norms," using hypothetical variations to see what the speakers felt would have happened had certain conditions been different (Hoebel 1954:41). For example, a Cheyenne man is expected to react with indifference if his wife leaves him for another man. What happened when Red Eagle beat and threatened to kill the "stealer" of his wife? (161–162). This "trouble" case method continues to play a major role in legal anthropology fieldwork.

THE CASE METHOD AND ITS DISCONTENTS

Llewellyn was trying to adapt the case method to societies that did not have written records (Llewellyn and Hoebel, 1941). After all, Llewellyn was a lawyer and studied law using the "case method." Lawyers in common-law countries like England and the United States are exposed to this method in law school. Just as they will do throughout their careers, they construct arguments on behalf of their clients by reading cases that have already been tried and ruled upon by the courts, thus providing a precedent for the outcome of future cases. It is important to remember, however, that the "cases" so important to those working in the common law are not full transcripts of proceedings, but instead they are brief summaries of the facts as seen by the judge, followed by consideration of relevant law, and concluding with a verdict. The cases reported by Llewellyn and Hoebel and their followers continue to use this model, but, as we shall see, some contemporary scholars question whether this is actually the best one for legal anthropology.

Because Hoebel and Llewellyn were interested in a culture that no longer existed, they were forced to rely on the memory of their elderly informants. The problems are obvious. Although people in nonliterate societies often cultivate their memories in ways that appear amazing to those who are able to fall back on the written word, even the best of memories can fail over time. Names are mistaken, dates confused, and relevant details slip away. The informant may have biases that are difficult to discern. There is also the danger that the informant is recounting things the way he feels they should have taken place in a past that the informant may be glorifying. And informants may sometimes say what they think the interviewer wants to hear. Hypothetical variations on reported cases present even greater dangers of eliciting ideal rather than real reactions.

Where possible, therefore, fieldworkers prefer to depend on cases that they have observed and recorded themselves. This method has its own problems. For one, it depends a great deal on luck—on being in the right place at the right time. People do not always arrange their disputes to fit the fieldworker's schedule. The fieldworker must also ask if the disputes and cases she witnessed were typical or representative of disputing behavior in that society. Where groups are small and disputes rare, it may be hard to collect enough cases to comprise a representative sample. Observed cases may be supplemented with hypothetical or memory cases, but these present the problems discussed above.

A different sort of reservation about the case system stems from the use that is made of it. Accustomed to the common-law tradition of studying cases for the purpose of finding applicable law, anthropologists used the cases they collected to identify the substantive and procedural law of the group they were studying. Although they often related aspects of law to other aspects of the culture, the case method assumed that law was a separate realm, one that could initially be studied in isolation. Some fieldworkers began to feel that what they had isolated as "the case" was actually merely one part of a tension that may have arisen years—or generations—earlier and that might continue to affect relations within the group for a long time to come.

Sally Falk Moore (1978) was instrumental in articulating the issues involved. She suggested that one way in which legal systems differed from each other was "in the degree to which 'private' disputes between individuals have potential political or structural importance" (91). With her own work with the Chagga of Tanzania, she demonstrated the ways in which private and public were often interlocked, and she showed that the personal dimensions of a dispute could have political origins and political repercussions. This approach adds the dimension of time to the study of law. It sees the dispute that comes to public attention as one slice of a process that may cover many decades. The dispute itself may provide an insight into which areas of the culture and social structure are under stress. Because this approach views the source and the consequences of the case as being as important as the case itself, it is usually referred to as the "extended case method." Although it has proven its value, it is necessary to point out that it has the same drawbacks as any other method that depends on the memories of other people.

Kritzer (2002) demonstrates some of the differences between relying on even recent memory and engaging in actual observation. In his study of contingency fee legal practice in Wisconsin, he spent a month in each of three law firms and also conducted a series of semi-structured interviews with contingency fee practitioners around the state. In comparing the two sets of data, he first notes the amount of detail that is lost when he uses interviews rather than observation. Perhaps more to the point, he found that in the interviews the lawyers stressed the amount of control that they have over their clients, while his observations indicated how hard lawyers work to satisfy their clients (153). Kritzer suggests that in interviews lawyers like to show how their knowledge of the legal system allows them to manage their clients; Kritzer's long hours spent in law offices, however, showed that lawyers are acutely aware that referrals help their practices thrive and that satisfied clients produce referrals. For example, one of the observed lawyers took a case about which he had some doubts simply because the client had been referred by a previous client; he hoped his efforts on behalf of the new client would in turn result in future referrals.

ANTHROPOLOGY AND ADVOCACY

A number of social scientists have felt an uncomfortable gap between their goals as researchers of law and cultures and the actual problems confronted by the people they are studying. In addition, the scholars are conscious that they often possess more wealth, power, or status than the people whose lives provide the data for their research. Anthropologists, in particular, are keenly aware that colonial regimes often used anthropological findings for their own ends. Some have embraced a feminist/Marxist orientation or the approach of critical legal studies, both of which encourage their followers not only to study power relationships, but also to change them. All of these motivations have driven many sociolegal scholars to develop research methods that include political engagement.

Susan Hirsch (2002:13–33) provides an interesting example. She used her research in Tanzania both to collect data on women's knowledge of and access to the legal system and, at the same time, to consciously increase Tanzanian women's understanding of the law. She began by using a number of standard methods of legal research—a review of case files from courts at different levels; interviews with legal personnel, law reform advocates, and laypeople with court experience; and the study of relevant scholarly and legal documents. Her next step was more unusual; she attended a weekly workshop hosted by a local feminist group seeking to increase "legal literacy" among women. The workshop provided an opportunity for group discussion, which she found to be a more fruitful data-collecting technique than one-on-one interviews; participating in the discussion also gave her occasions to share her information about the workings of the Tanzanian legal system and ways in which other women had made the legal system work for them.

BEYOND THE BOUNDS OF VILLAGE AND COURT

Another factor driving anthropologists to methodological innovations is globalization and speedy communication. Ideas—including legal ideas—are developed in one place, communicated to others, put into practice in yet others, and feedback from that practice returns to where the ideas were originally developed. Anthropologists aware of these circumstances find themselves frustrated when they confine themselves to study in one village or town.

Mark Goodale (2002:50–71) confronted this situation when he became aware of the impact of Western human rights discourse on rural Bolivia. Starting in the 1990s, most Bolivians came to accept the central premise that the nation contained distinct groups of citizens identified as "indigenous" and that these groups had special rights. This premise did not originate in Bolivia, but was a direct result of specific proclamations of international groups such as the United Nations and its working bodies, specifically the International Labor Organization. During this same period, a great number of international nongovernmental organizations (NGOs) came to rural Bolivia to help implement legal reform. These groups also used the language of human rights.

As Goodale observed cases in Bolivian hamlets and small kin-based settlements, he found the language and concepts of human

rights playing an ever-larger part. He would not be able to understand these new and constantly shifting "legal ideas" by remaining
in a courtroom or village, but would have to track them "from, to
and within rural Bolivia" (64). He interviewed NGO representatives
throughout the province as well as in other parts of the country,
including their headquarters in the nation's capital. He followed
union workers from one meeting to another as they agitated for
workers' rights and then to the regional center where they learned
more human rights doctrine. Goodale realized that the legal ideas
that were the center of his research were also to be found in documents, so he went to Sucre, the nation's legal capital, and to offices
and libraries in the relevant state capital. He deplored that lack of
money prevented him from following these legal ideas back to
Europe and the United States. Although Goodale continued to make
use of participant observation and interviewing, this "multisited"
approach to ethnography allowed him to understand how legal
ideas operate in an ever-shrinking world.

THE WORDS OF JUSTICE

Another method available to legal anthropologists has its origins in linguistics, in the study of language. The "cases" reported by
fieldworkers are rarely full transcriptions of proceedings but are
instead synopses of the facts as presented by disputants and witnesses, together with summaries of the proceeding and the outcome. Translations or transcriptions of the participants' actual
words may be included, but they rarely comprise more than a frac-
tion of the report. Fieldworkers may unconsciously model their
reports after those used by lawyers. Often the fieldworker does not
have a strong enough command of the language or the stenographic
skills to provide a fuller account. While recording machines may
help to alleviate this problem, they introduce others. For example,
recorders make some people uneasy, while others flatly refuse to
speak in front of them. Transcription of recordings is time-consuming, tedious, and often costly. Including full transcriptions of a representative number of cases would produce a book longer than most
publishers would want to publish or most readers would want to
read. While many of anthropology's traditional questions can be
answered by traditional reports, anthropologists working in the

subfield of linguistics have opened up new areas of study (Brenneis and Meyers 1984). Conley and O'Barr (1998) examine several areas of law, demonstrating in each instance how linguistic analysis reveals the nature of law's power and its inequality of application, even when legal rules and procedures display no discrimination. Their work suggests that this is true across time and place.

Laurence Goldman (1986) provides a striking example of what happens when the anthropologist works from the actual words rather than from summaries and treats those words with the methods developed by linguists. Goldman worked with the Huli people of Papua New Guinea. The Huli traditionally handled many disputes in informal public forums referred to as *moots*. Huli women were generally socially inferior to men, but the moots were perceived as an exception to this, since women could bring their grievances to the moot and could act as witnesses and supporters, with no restraints on their testimony or on how they presented it. However, when Goldman examined the actual discourse of the moot, he found subtle but real gender discrimination. For example, questions put to women— far more frequently than those put to men—took the form of a statement with a rising tone at the end. A moot mediator would ask a man "Were you asleep?" To a woman, it would be "You were asleep?" The former is neutral and is equally receptive to a positive or a negative answer. In the latter instance, the woman who was not asleep is forced to contradict the questioner. Goldman also found that women were more often given questions that could be answered with a simple "yes" or "no," while men tended to get open-ended questions that required longer, detailed answers allowing the men to demonstrate their narrative skills. Goldman suggests that it is the style of questioning that reveals gender inequality and that style is lost when scholars do not understand how the nuances of the verbal and nonverbal language used in legal matters affect the outcomes.

NOT ONLY ANTHROPOLOGISTS

Although the emphasis thus far has been on the methods developed by anthropologists, members of other disciplines have found their own ways to study the relationships between law and culture. Political scientists studying contemporary cultures often focus intently on a small number of related cases and their effects on the political situation. Stuart Scheingold (1988) shows how resistance to school integration demanded by the decision in *Brown v. Board of Education* (1954) led to the formation of the civil rights movement. Lisa Bower (1994) demonstrates that *Bowers v. Hardwick* (1986), in which the Supreme Court of the United States decided that the right to privacy did not extend to consensual sodomy, was one of the factors leading to a new stage in gay and lesbian activism.

Biographers also have made contributions to the understanding of the association between law and culture. An early and outstanding example is Catherine Drinker Bowen's *The Lion and the Throne,* a biography of Sir Edward Coke, attorney general and chief justice of England during the reigns of Elizabeth I and James I (1957). She shows the role that Coke played in defending the fundamental principles of common law—free speech, the right to a public trial, the writ of habeas corpus. Historians, making use of written records, are able to trace events over long periods of time. In *The Making of the Civil Law* (1981) Alan Watson argues that the difference between civil and common-law systems is due more to legal history than to political or economic forces and that it was the acceptance of the authority of Roman law that shaped the various systems of civil law.

COMBINING METHODS

Many contemporary students of law and culture refuse to confine themselves to one method. In *Colonizing Hawaii* (2000) Sally Engle Merry combines the questions and concepts of anthropologists with the documentary expertise of historians to trace the role that law played in changing Hawaii from an independent kingdom to an American colony. She uses court records combined with contemporary ethnography to illuminate the way law changed everyday life in the realms of family, work, and sexual activity, under the banner of bringing civilization and progress to the indigenous people of the islands.

Merry's book provides an excellent example of one of the major trends in the study of law and culture—the tendency to borrow freely and to combine whatever methods seem best suited to answering the questions being posed and the hypotheses being tested. This cross-fertilization of methods promises to make the study of law and culture an even more vibrant field than it already is.

Notes

[1] Fortes, Meyer. 1945. *The Dynamics of Clanship Among the Tallensi.* London: Oxford University Press; Nadel, S. F. 1956. "Reason and Unreason in African Law. *African* 26:160–173; Evans-Pritchard, E. E. 1940. *The Nuer.* Oxford: Clarendon Press.

[2] Gluckman, Max, 1955. *The Judicial Process Among the Barotse of Northern Rhodesia.* Manchester: Manchester University Press; Gulliver, P. H. 1963. *Social Control in an African Society.* Boston: Boston University Press; Turner, Victor. 1957. *Schism and Continuity in an African Society.* Manchester: Manchester University Press.

Chapter Three

Typology

Every country has its own legal system; indeed, one of the definitions of nationhood is the acknowledged existence of a legal system within a defined border. But as we shall see, many countries are comprised of different groups that have their own legal system, so these countries have more than one legal system. In addition, legal systems change over time in ways both great and small. The student of law and culture rapidly realizes that even the most superficial study of all or even most of these systems is impossible. One solution to this problem is to confine oneself to one culture and to study it in as much depth as time allows. These *legal ethnographies* are often based upon long periods of fieldwork and painstaking analyses of the relationships between specific aspects of the legal system and their cultural contexts.

These ethnographies provide the data necessary for two other solutions to this problem, both of which involve the *comparative* approach. The first involves studying a group of closely related legal systems and trying to account for their differences. This is the approach often used in comparative law courses in law school. The second comparative solution calls for the study of a small number of legal systems, each one being somehow representative of many others. This is the approach used in this text, but it immediately presents another problem: Representative in what way? Solving this problem demands that legal systems be divided into groups with group membership based on one or more shared characteristics. Such a set of groups is called a *typology*. It is then possible to compare a small number of systems from each of the groups.

The characteristics involved in building a typology often depend on the questions or interests of the person building it. In the case of legal systems, the person designing the typology might choose geography as a variable for grouping and comparing legal systems—all the legal systems of a continent, perhaps. Or time—the legal system of England in different centuries—might be the basis of the typography. As another example, it could be based on forms of government—democracy, chieftainship, theocracy, band, republic, monarchy, and socialist. Another possibility would concern the nature of the decision makers—are they full-time legal specialists, political officeholders, priests, or a gathering of elders? Obviously, the variables on which legal systems could be grouped are numerous.

The variables given here as examples are not necessarily mutually exclusive. It is possible to place nineteenth-century African chieftainships in one group and nineteenth-century Arab Islamic states in another, with nineteenth-century Asian monarchies comprising a third. Of course, it would also be possible to divide the nineteenth-century African chieftainships into East and West African chieftainships and the Asian monarchies into East and South Asian monarchies.

This short discussion of typologies should make two things very clear. First, typologies are not found in nature; scholars create them for their own purposes. Second, typologies can be very simple or very complex. Complex typologies contain many groups, each of which has few members with a great deal in common. Simple typologies have few groups, each of which has many members with perhaps only one relevant thing in common. This text, for example, utilizes an extremely simple typology, one that looks at legal systems only in terms of the source of the law.

More precisely, the typology used in this text is based on what its followers believe to be the source of the law. The source of the law is important, for this is what gives any particular law as well as the entire legal system its legitimacy. Concentrating on law's source—its origin—produces a typology that puts most of the world's legal systems for the most part into one of three categories, albeit categories with very fuzzy boundaries: (1) Western law, (2) religious law, and (3) traditional (or customary) law. Two other categories—socialist law and Eastern law—have historically influenced nations as well and have their own distinctive features.

Although the defining characteristics of each category will be described more thoroughly in the chapter devoted to it, the following is a brief explanation of the groupings in this typology.

A SIMPLE TYPOLOGY

Western law begins with two major subgroups. One contains the legal systems of the European continent. Although there are many differences among European legal systems, they all are descended from the law of the Roman Empire and were influenced by the procedures of Medieval Roman Catholic canon law. This subgroup is often referred to as the *civil law* tradition. The other subgroup is English *common law*. Because both England and many European countries imposed their legal systems on their colonies, today we find Western law as the dominant influence in Latin America, North America, Africa, Australia, New Zealand, and some nations in Asia. Although there are major differences among the legal systems of these nations, they have in common what they perceive as the source of their laws.

Western law is human law and it is state law. That means that the humans who make Western law are officials of the state. They may be hereditary monarchs or nobles, they may be elected representatives, or they may be appointees of one of the former. In any case, it is their positions as government officials that give their legal pronouncements legitimacy.

These pronouncements take two forms. Officials may *make* law; they announce new rules or change old rules. This is often referred to as *legislation*. But officials may also *find* law; that is, they interpret exiting rules, policies, documents, or traditions to apply to present circumstances. The fact is, Western law is made by human beings. Western law is secular and neither gods nor ancestors are consulted or insulted when it is altered. This means that Western law can change quickly when circumstances change.

For example, English landowners had for centuries "entailed" their estates, meaning they bequeathed them to their male heirs under the condition that the land could not be sold but would be transferred intact to the next generation. Landowners lived on the rents of their tenant farmers. In the 1860s, Cyrus McCormick introduced the mechanical reaper, a machine that harvested the wheat of America's Great Plains at half the cost of hand labor, thus halving the cost of producing and consequently the price of wheat. While English city dwellers delighted in the vastly reduced price of bread, English tenant farmers received vastly lower prices for their crops and were unable to pay their rents and as a result, English landowners found themselves with vastly reduced incomes. Desperate for cash, landowners persuaded Parliament to pass the Settled Lands Acts of 1882 and 1884, permitting the owners of entailed estates to sell their land (Lacey 1998:40–41). Some tenant farmers were able to buy the formerly rented land at low prices; others were evicted by new landlords.

Admirers of Western law believe that it is rational, formulated as the result of careful consideration of the public good, and flexible to meet the needs of a rapidly changing world; its detractors suggest that it can be easily formulated to meet the needs of the wealthy and powerful. The Settled Lands Acts illustrate both points of view.

Hindus, Jews, and Muslims believe that the god or gods they worship gave their law to them. There are a number of implications to this. The first is that mere humans cannot change divine law; this gives *religious law* a stability that Western law lacks, but it also makes it difficult to adapt religious law to changing circumstances. A second implication is that those who are best able to understand and apply religious law are religious scholars and religious officials. This means that where a state adopts religious law, state and religion are the same organization or, at the very least, inextricably intertwined. A third implication is that breaking a religious law is an offense against the divine as well as against the community or a particular individual. This raises the question of how secular punishments coordinate with divine punishments administered in this life or in the hereafter.

Among the few nations that use religious law as their primary law are Iran and Saudi Arabia, both of which use *shariah* or Islamic law exclusively. The constitutions of most countries on the Persian Gulf identify shariah law as a source or the "main source" of their legislation. Other countries may use religious law for certain aspects of their legal system; most Islamic countries, for example, use shariah law as personal status law—rules about marriage, divorce, and inheritance. Article 1 of the Egyptian Civil Code directs judges to look to Muslim law in cases where the code has no applicable law. In Nigeria, several states with a majority Muslim population have adopted Islamic law, although in practice it is often mixed with local customary law. Israel's legal system is based on Western law although courts for Jews, Muslims, Druze, and Christians apply relevant religious laws in matters of marriage and divorce. Decisions of these courts are subject to Israeli law and appealable to the nation's supreme court. Political parties wishing to make greater use of Jewish law in other areas serve in the legislature where they vie with parties wishing for a more secular legal system.

Traditional or *customary* law differs from the other categories of law mainly in the fact that it relies heavily on rules and precedents that are *unwritten.* Although all the legal systems being considered in this text have roots in custom and morality, traditional law relies on these more heavily. It tends to be less technical than other types of law and to place more emphasis on the rights of the group than on the rights of the individual. Traditional legal systems rarely have full-time legal specialists such as judges and lawyers. Where third parties are involved, they may be elders, chiefs, religious authorities, or people who have kinship ties with all parties to the dispute. There may be more concern with restitution and reintegration than with punishment or some abstract notion of justice. Today no nations rely exclusively on customary law, but many nations incorporate it in some way. Principles of customary law may be codified in legislation or they may provide precedents in case law. Indigenous groups may practice part or all of their traditional law, although they are embedded in nations practicing some other type of law. Most intriguing, many Western law nations are showing interest in the techniques of restitution, reconciliation, mediation, and reintegration of the offender, which are the hallmarks of customary law.

Socialist law fits uneasily into this typology. Although many legal scholars find it distinctive enough to warrant a separate category (David and Brierley 1985), this text joins others (Quigley 1989) in grouping it with the civil-law tradition and thus an instance of Western law. Most socialist law clearly shows its civil-law underpinnings; what makes it important today are the changes in law taking place especially as formerly socialist countries, such as Poland and Hungary, partially or totally integrate free market principles into their economies. The People's Republic of China maintains a socialist legal system while it also attempts to incorporate free enterprise. A brief look at socialist law may help in understanding its relevance to other types of law.

After the Russian Revolution of 1917, the victorious Communist Party wanted to do away with the legal system based on that of the European continent and substitute one based on socialist philosophy. What actually happened in Russia, as well as in other socialist states such as those of Eastern Europe, the People's Republic of China, Vietnam, and Cuba, was the addition of certain socialist principles to the existing civil law copied from or imposed by European nations.

The most important of these principles is that law is an instrument of governmental policy; the purpose of law is to support certain political and economic goals. Primary among these is the protection of the socialist state and its collectivized economy.

> Law in a capitalist economy tells its citizens to observe the rules of justice and morality and, as a result, the society will enjoy economic order. Socialist law says it will help provide the desirable order and the result will be justice and morality for all the citizens. The complete reversal of attitudes toward law brings a total transformation of fundamental ideas about law. (Reichel 1999:100–101)

The judiciary is not expected to be independent but is considered to be a vital partner to other arms of government in developing and enforcing socialism. Finally, socialists emphasize the educational value of law; public trials and punishments are not for the protection of the defendant, but to clarify for onlookers the content of the law and the consequences of offending.

While socialist nations emphasize the difference between their legal system and that of nonsocialist nations, students of comparative law tend to see differences of degree. Socialists themselves condemn the legal systems of capitalist countries as supporting capitalist economic policy and the social status quo; indeed, they accuse capitalist countries of hypocrisy, claiming that capitalism only pretends to provide opportunity for economic advancement. Similarly, all legal systems recognize that they educate as well as dispense justice and mediate disputes. Socialist legal systems are unique primarily because they articulate some principles about which other systems are silent.

A final category of law to be considered here is *Eastern law*. This is the philosophy of law that has influenced most of the countries of

Asia, including China and Japan. Its foundation is the teachings of the Chinese sage and political theorist Confucius (K'ung Fu-tzu 551–479 BC). It is true that the contemporary law of these nations is usually based on Western law—common, civil, or socialist—and reflects decades and in some cases centuries of independent development. But the legal processes and cultures of these countries reflect their Confucian heritage sufficiently to make the study of Confucian law worthwhile. In addition, the Confucian attitude toward law and the legal system contrasts so directly with that of the West that it provides a valuable counterpoint.

Until the end of the nineteenth century, the term "rule of law" had a negative connotation in China. According to Confucius, rulers should govern by behaving correctly themselves, by setting a good example. Lower government officials would follow this example and village officials would follow the examples set by members of the central government. Finally, the example would be passed down to family heads, who would convey it to the members of their households. Of course, example alone was never considered a sufficient means of inculcating correct behavior. Studying Confucian principles of virtue was also important and comprised a large percentage of the educational system from the earliest school years and throughout the lifetime. Immersed in the principles of correct behavior and surrounded by people who practiced them, the Chinese child would grow into an adult who had internalized virtue and behaved in the proper fashion because that was the right thing to do. "Law," with its connotations of detailed rules and punishment for misbehavior, indicated that the rulers of the nation had ceased to set a good example or that the educational system had failed.

Chinese people, did, of course, have disputes and disagreements. Confucian ethics called for these to be settled privately, perhaps by involving a third party. If the disputants did bring their problem to court, the assumption was that that both of them were stubborn, uncompromising people who were unable to sacrifice their personal interests for the peace of the community. Court proceedings were so unpleasant most people tried to avoid them at all costs.

If a dispute were brought before a judge, however, he would not turn to law books for a solution. The term "rule of law," which makes Westerners think in terms of equality and impartiality, dismayed Confucians, who felt that no two instances were ever identical. To apply the same law to cases that were different could only result in injustice. The solution, according to Confucian theory, was to choose as judges learned men of wisdom and integrity and to give them great discretion in deciding cases. Confucians felt most comfortable with a legal system directed by the "rule of men."

MULTIPLE SYSTEMS OF LAW

In many nations, several different legal systems coexist—sometimes harmoniously, sometimes not. For Westerners, the first examples that may come to mind are countries with federal systems of government. Canada, the United States, Australia, and Germany, to mention a few, are nations in which laws may differ from state to state or province to province, and each may differ from the laws of the central government. In these instances it is the *content* of the laws that may differ; in each case, the legal *system* is still that of Western law.

A slightly more complex situation involves one legal system incorporating rules or institutions from another. In the Canadian province of Quebec and in the Northwest Territories, for example, the Western legal system recognizes the Inuit traditional institution of adoption in which a mother may "give" a child to a relative or other community member to raise without benefit of bureaucracy or paperwork. This option is open only to Inuit people, not to other Canadians (Yerbury and Griffiths 1999).

LEGAL PLURALISM

Greater difficulties arise when a country attempts to maintain separate legal systems for various ethnic groups. This situation is often called *legal pluralism*—"the coexistence of different normative orders within one socio-political space" (von Benda-Beckman 1997:1). Legal pluralism is sometimes the legacy of colonialism. The colonizing power would impose its own system of law on the indigenous people or, at least, override decisions of traditional law if those decisions did not reflect the colonizers' values or meet their wishes. As the former colonies gained their independence, they usually retained the Western legal system of colonial times, a system often administered by former colonialists or by a Western-educated native elite. Today, many former colonies in Africa, Australia, and the Americas find themselves with several distinct populations with different legal needs. Citizens of European descent, urbanites, highly educated people, and those in business or the professions are content with a legal system of Western derivation. Not only do they have easy access to police, lawyers, and courts, but they also find such a legal system to be in accord with their values of individual rights, abstract justice, and explicit rules that apply equally to all in the community. Indigenous people, on the other hand, often live in remote rural areas where representatives of the government's legal system are seldom seen. That legal system is not designed for their foraging or horticultural or public welfare economies. Furthermore, Western law does not reflect their emphasis on the rights of the community, the need for conflict resolution and the restoration of social harmony, reintegration of offenders, and a flexibility that is lost when laws and cases are written down and become constraining precedents.

Nevertheless, practicality and cultural congruity alone do not explain indigenous people's increasing demand for their own legal systems. This demand for a separate—or customized—legal system is also a way of asserting their identity and refusing to accept the control of the colonial powers and their Westernized successors. This control is often called *hegemony*, the disproportionate influence of one nation over another. By maintaining their right to their own legal systems and by establishing such systems with or without government approval, indigenous people attempt to carve out an area of their lives that is free of foreign domination.

In Canada, the government has tried to accommodate First Nations citizens by hiring them as special constables or court workers. This does nothing, however, to change the legal system and continues federal government control over native peoples. In response, a number of native communities have created their own community-based programs including police forces and alternatives to the government justice system, alternatives that often utilize customary law. Most of these initiatives receive no recognition by the federal government (Yerbury and Griffiths 1999: 26–44).

Donna Van Cott (2003) gives Latin American examples of several ways in which indigenous legal systems coexist—sometimes quite uneasily—with the Western-derived governmental systems.

In remote areas where the state does not penetrate, indigenous people handle most cases of dispute or deviance by traditional means. Closer to urban centers, they remit serious cases, such as homicide, or cases involving foreigners to the government system, for fear of being prosecuted themselves for overstepping their bounds. Serious cases may also be yielded to the state when the community has given up on reintegrating the offender. Latin American traditional systems also reflect the influence of governmental Western law systems in other ways. They are sensitive to accusations of human rights abuse, especially since indigenous people often phrase their own complaints against the government in human rights terms. They look to governmental legal systems when confronted with situations with which their own system has no experience. They may sanction deviants by threatening to bring them to the state system. And they may strive for legitimacy by writing down their decisions and registering and codifying their norms—perhaps depriving themselves of the very flexibility that has been a hallmark of traditional law (Van Cott 2003:6).

The political status of indigenous systems varies from country to country and from time to time. The southern African nation of Botswana provides an interesting example of ongoing changes in the relationship between Western and indigenous law. In 1885 the British declared the territory that is today Botswana to be the British Protectorate of Bechuanaland; this meant that Britain would protect the area against foreign invasion but would not involve itself in internal administration and would not disturb the customary system of law and justice. The British did insist, however, that British subjects in Bechuanaland be tried by British courts using British law. This meant that there was a dual legal system. Traditional courts applied traditional law to the majority of the population, people who identified with the culture of the indigenous Tswana people. Other courts applied European law to "Europeans" (including children of Europeans who were actually born in Africa), other foreigners, and native people whose education or occupation made them unwilling to be governed by customary law. This racially separate system was in effect when Bechuanaland became the independent Republic of Botswana in 1966.

Today's dual system reflects culture rather than race. There is one set of courts—Statutory Courts—that applies what is sometimes called "formal law," that is, the nation's legal codes, legislation passed by its Parliament, and the decisions of judges; they are presided over by trained judges. Customary Courts, on the other hand, make use of Tswana traditional law, and chiefs and elders hand down judgments. But this picture of two totally separate court systems is misleading.

Customary Courts may not try certain kinds of cases, murder being the most prominent, and their decisions may be appealed to the higher Statutory Courts. Statutory Courts are encouraged to apply traditional law in cases where it is "properly applied," while Customary Courts may apply formal law where they think appropriate. Although Botswana is short of formally educated legal personnel, there is nothing to stop lawyers from appearing in Customary Courts and these courts are supposed to keep written records. The stated goal is a merged legal system that will apply both formal law and customary law. Meanwhile, Botswanans of any race may litigate in whichever court seems most favorable to their particular circumstances.

This short description of the court structure of Botswana shows that even the simple typology described earlier cannot account for all of the world's legal systems. Some, such as Confucian China, do not fit comfortably into any category while others, such contemporary Botswana, combine several categories.

LEGAL PLURALISM AS THE NORM

Colonialism is not the only source of legal pluralism. Immigrant groups may use their own legal system to regulate relationships between members (von Benda-Beckman and Strijbosch 1986). Nation-states have expanded, incorporating within their borders groups that were formerly autonomous and that have attempted to retain their legal systems. Institutions such as arbitration, negotiation, and facilitation keep many disputes out of courtrooms. "Consequently, plurality of legal systems now appears to be a fundamental characteristic of all societies, not only those with colonial histories" (Merry 1992:358).

This expanded view of legal pluralism is also due to the growing role of international law and international treaties. Transnational corporations, the World Bank, the International Monetary Fund, the North American Free Trade Agreement, plus treaties regulating copyrights and patents add new types of law at both national and local levels (Ghai, Luckham, and Snyder 1987:275). Mark Galanter (1986) gives the example of the 1984 disastrous leakage of poison gas into a squatter settlement in Bhopal, India. Because the factory involved was partially owned by an American corporation, it set off a furious debate as to where the subsequent lawsuit should be heard and which country's laws should decide it. The American corporation denied any involvement and wanted the case to be heard in India. However, Indian tort law (laws about civil wrongs) was relatively undeveloped and most tort cases were tried as criminal cases, resulting in long delays and rules unfavorable to those claiming that they were victims. The case was ultimately settled out of court in India, but not before India's courts had made some decisions that involved adopting laws developed in England and America.

The pervasiveness of legal pluralism shows that the typology that begins this chapter is a place to start the study of law, not to end it. It is the relationship *among* different legal orders in the same space—whether that be a village, a nation, a courtroom, a commercial venture, or a multinational enterprise—that occupies the attention of many contemporary scholars of law.

Chapter Four

Western Law

HISTORY

The process and methods of law and justice in the Western world have continually evolved during the course of history. A thousand years ago the accused would be bound and thrown into a river or pond. Why? Since both God and water prized purity and rejected sin, an innocent person would sink, while a guilty one would float to the surface. Or the accused might be burnt with hot metal and the wound bandaged; signs of healing within three days showed that God was protecting an innocent person from harm. Or perhaps accuser and accused would fight a duel, the audience being confident that God would give victory to the truthful one. To make sure that all was carried out properly—and perhaps to call God's attention to the test being conducted—a Roman Catholic priest would preside over the events.

These were the common forms of determining truth in early Medieval Europe. Faith in God and in God's willingness to protect the innocent underlay faith in trial by ordeal or by battle. It came as a shock, therefore, when in AD 1215, the Roman Catholic Church forbade its priests to take part in any of these proceedings.

No one is quite sure why the Fourth Lateran Council, called by Pope Innocent III, should suddenly abandon methods that had proven satisfactory for centuries. Since other measures of the council addressed the integrity of the priesthood, it may be that priests

41

had been taking bribes to determine the outcome of ordeals. It is also possible that people were noticing cases in which the results of battle or ordeal were discredited by later evidence or confessions. In any case, both the continent of Europe and the island of England were forced to find new ways to settle disputes before the law—and to find them quickly.

At this point the continent and the island went their separate ways. The diverse duchies and principalities of Europe turned to the one institution that united them—the Catholic Church. The Church had its own body of law—canon law—and a well-developed set of procedures to carry it out. Because priests were literate, canon law was systematically written down and its procedures tended to rely on written records. When all available evidence had been reduced to writing and placed in a *dossier*, it was placed before one or more priests who were well versed in law and who would render a decision based on it. Oral testimony in court, if heard at all, was merely supplementary to the dossier. This became the model for the law and the courts of the European continent.

Deprived of ordeal and battle, England went in another direction. It embraced a secular institution that had always existed side-by-side with the Church-sanctioned alternatives: *compurgation* or wager of law. When there was doubt about the truthfulness of a person's statement, he would be asked to swear an oath. He would then bring friends, neighbors, and kinsmen to swear that they believed him. These *oath-helpers* were character references rather than witnesses; they did not swear that they knew the facts of the matter but rather that they did not think that the person in question would lie. If two people presented different versions of the facts, each might be asked to round up oath-helpers. The person with the largest number of supporters was judged to be the most truthful. Centuries later, the oath-helpers would evolve into the English jury.

The foregoing illustrates two points to keep in mind as we examine Western law. The first is that what is referred to as Western law consists of two branches that were originally quite different from each other. The *civil law* branch is found today in the countries of the European continent and in many of the nations that were formerly their colonies. *Common law* is practiced in England and most of her former colonies. In spite of these differences, it is the similarities that become more and more striking as time goes on. The second point is that Western law, which is characterized as law made by human beings, actually has deep roots in both religion and custom. Religion and custom have influenced Western law in the past and continue to do so today. Nevertheless, it is the human role in making law that distinguishes both branches of Western law from the other types of law considered here.

SOURCES OF CIVIL LAW

The law of the European continent, or civil law, traces itself back to the law of ancient Rome. Roman judges relied on custom and on the laws passed by the Roman Senate, but when faced with difficult cases they turned to a group of men known as *jurisconsults*. Jurisconsults were scholars of the law who often advised judges, thereby staying close to the actual problems presented in courts. Their opinions were collected and the principles derived from them were compiled into treatises—books that were read by anyone who wished to become knowledgeable about law. Three aspects of civil law were already apparent: the interest in abstract principles, the role of scholars, and the importance of writing.

The Roman Empire spread the influence of Roman law over much of the civilized world, an early example of law being spread via imperialism. With the Empire's decline, however, much of that influence was diluted, with Roman and customary law being thoroughly mixed and quite different from one area to the next.

By the year 1000, trade and travel across the continent had stabilized to the extent that Europeans felt the need of a predictable and efficient institution for settling disputes. The Roman treatises had been lost by then, but what was available was one of the great law books of all times—the *Corpus Juris Civilis*, compiled by the Byzantine Emperor Justinian in the sixth century. It was from the title of this collection of Roman laws that European law became known as civil law. Its content provided the basis for what would become the law of Europe and much of the rest of the world.

With the fall of the Roman Empire in the years from AD 300 to 400, the Roman Catholic Church took on some of the functions of government. It had always claimed jurisdiction over priests and members of holy orders, but during the Middle Ages its tribunals also acquired jurisdiction over matrimonial matters, inheritance, and some aspects of criminal law. Both the substance and procedures of these areas of canon law would find their way into the secular law of Europe.

Commercial law also provided material for the civil law. As Europe emerged from the localism of the Middle Ages, it developed prosperous trade routes over land and sea. Towns and markets grew into major commercial centers, sprouting important markets and banks. Neither Roman nor canon law provided mechanisms for the speedy settlement of business matters, so guilds and associations of merchants developed their own rules and their own tribunals to enforce them. These rules, based on the "custom and usage" of artisans and merchants, proved so effective that the "law merchant" would be applied by government courts; it would transcend international boundaries and was the one area of civil law to find favor in England.

In the sixteenth century, many of the small duchies and principalities of Europe started coming together into bodies that we would recognize as nation-states. Each nation began to develop its own distinct culture. Vernacular languages replaced Latin in the universities and in literature. National, rather than European, schools of art and music came into being. New varieties of Christianity arose to challenge Roman Catholicism. Law was also subjected to this new nationalism. Newly formed central governments encouraged legal scholars to pull together these various sources of law and combine them with the traditions of their own regions. The result of this was codification, the attempt to produce a "rational, systematized and comprehensive legal system" that would not only bring order to the chaos of existing law but would also ensure the centrality of the state in the law-making process (Glendon, Gordon, and Carozza 1999:32). Although the lawmakers would respect the old sources of law, they need not necessarily find them binding.

This meant that codes could be tools of change as well as tools of stability. The French Civil Code of 1804 (often referred to as the Code Napoleon) embodied the egalitarian values of the French revolution. In order to break down the great estates of the old nobility, the code made it easier to buy and sell land, limited inheritances, introduced the institution of adoption, and permitted divorce by mutual consent. At the same time, it continued to protect private property and the power of the husband and father in the traditional family.

SOURCES OF COMMON LAW

The Roman legacy of abstract principles, writing, codification, and the importance of scholarship did not reach across the English Channel. Contemporary common law finds its earliest roots in the feudal system of the Middle Ages (c. 500–1500.) Feudalism was a socioeconomic pyramid. The king was the head of the pyramid, theoretically owning all the land of the country. He allotted some land to his nobles, who owed him loyalty in return. The nobles in turn allocated their land among people of lesser status. At the bottom of the pyramid were the peasants, who worked the land but had no rights to it. The inevitable disputes that arose in any community might be decided by a higher-ranking noble or could be taken to a court of the shire (county). In some disputes the facts were immediately evident and the custom of the area clear to all; when these circumstances were not met, courts resorted to trial by battle, ordeal, or oath-helpers. Recall that oath-helpers were friends, relatives, and neighbors of the litigants—a group of peers. Like most litigants of the time, they were uneducated and illiterate.

When William the Conqueror became ruler of England in 1066, he did not abolish the existing courts but added a system of royal courts. These were primarily designed to settle disputes among nobles. These national courts not only permitted a more consistent administration of justice but also gave more control to the king and allowed him to pocket the fees and fines collected by the courts. However, the king soon found that he did not have a monopoly on justice for the upper classes, as the Roman Catholic Church had its own courts and insisted on trying offenses against religion, which included adultery and incest, as well as family issues such as marriage and inheritance. Church personnel charged with crimes could claim "benefit of clergy" and have their cases moved to Church courts.

While justice for nobles was being made more efficient, local courts continued to administer justice for commoners according to local custom, custom that varied greatly from one place to another. However, many commoners soon preferred to take their cases to the royal courts whenever they had a choice. They perceived procedure there as being more fair than in the king's courts, and, perhaps even more important, these courts made use of neither battle nor ordeal.

Each case that went to a royal court deprived the local landowner of a fee and served to centralize the system of justice. By 1215—coincidentally the year of the Fourth Lateran Council—king and nobles signed the *Magna Carta*, which reduced the criminal jurisdiction of local courts. The Statute of Gloucester followed this in 1278, which severely restrained their civil jurisdiction. The centralized royal courts had, for all practical purposes, replaced the local courts.

The judges of this centralized court system decided cases by referring to custom, but they had to face the fact that courts in different parts of the country had been referring to different customs. The first major attempt to find common customs and turn them into "common law" is attributed a thirteenth-century judge named Henry de Bracton. Bracton searched the records of several courts, looking for cases that relied on the same custom. That custom and the cases that illustrated it were made available to other judges. Decisions were still based on custom, not cases, but cases were evidence of the custom. By the sixteenth century, judges were regularly citing prior cases in their decisions and in the seventeenth century decisions from the court of the state chancellor were held to be binding on other courts. The nineteenth century saw a reorganization of the courts with a single court of appeals, guaranteeing that the same body of law would be applied nationally. At the same time, elected legislators enacted large numbers of *statutes,* laws that might be based on custom, but might also depart from it radically.

DIFFERENCES WITHIN WESTERN LAW

This history of the role of *precedent* is also the history of one of the main differences between civil and common law. Legislatures in civil law countries enact legal *codes* (a systematic arrangement of laws designed to cover an entire legal area) and each judge refers directly to the code when deciding a case. Common law legislatures pass *statutes* (law written to address a specific legal situation) and judges look at the law itself as well as at the ways in which other judges have interpreted that law in previous cases. The decisions of the previous judges become binding, so that each judge applies the law in the same way.

Another difference between the two traditions is found in the way in which they arrive at the facts of a case. The civil law, with its respect for writing, relies on a *dossier,* a written record of the evidence compiled by neutral investigators under the direction of a neutral judge. Judges who have not been involved in the investigation (the number of judges depends on the seriousness of the case) receive the completed dossier and make their decision based on the evidence presented in it. The judges may call witnesses for clarification, but not for any new information that is not recorded in the dossier. In contrast, the common law, with its history of peers swearing publicly to what they know of the facts and the character of the litigants, relies far more on oral testimony given in the courtroom. Written material is entered into the record only under special circumstances.

This leads to what may be the most noticeable difference between the two families of Western law. The civil law utilizes the *inquisitorial* method while the common law utilizes the *adversarial* method. The former depends upon objective investigators who assemble all available evidence, regardless of which party it favors. This evidence is then presented to judges especially trained to evaluate such evidence and then apply appropriate law. The adversarial method depends on lawyers for the parties (defendant on the one hand, state or plaintiff on the other) to gather and present the evidence most favorable to their own side while looking for weaknesses in the evidence presented by their opponents. This evidence is not presented to a specially trained bench of judges but to a jury of laypersons selected from the community. It is they who will decide the facts of the case, while the judge decides only questions of law.

This division of labor between judge (finder of law) and jury (finder of fact) reflects a further difference between the two systems. The civil law system places great emphasis on the role of highly trained professionals. The career of judge is quite separate from that of attorney. Would-be judges attend schools that are entirely distinct from those attended by would-be attorneys, and they begin their careers as judges directly upon   graduation.

The common law relies far more heavily on the layperson and values experience at least as much as it values education. The clearest evidence of this is the presence of the jury, a body meant to be representative of the community. Not only are jurors not required to have legal training, in many jurisdictions too much legal knowledge may serve to disqualify a juror. Common-law judges have the same legal training as attorneys and usually begin their careers as attorneys. Once elected or appointed as judges, they may be sent for brief initiation and training programs, but they will learn most of what they need to know through experience. An even greater departure from the civil law's emphasis on education and professionalism can be found in the common law's reliance on lay magistrates or justices of the peace. This institution traces its history to the Justices of the Peace Act 1361, which granted "knights, esquires or gentlemen" of the area authority to "pursue, arrest, take, and chastise" those breaching the peace (Glendon, Gordon, and Carozza 1999:160). Today England and Wales have approximately 29,000 lay justices whose cases involve "summary" or minor offenses; these comprise about 95% of all criminal cases. The United States, as well as Canada and other nations of the British Commonwealth, also continue to make use of justices or lay magistrates who usually have no formal legal training at all.

SIMILARITIES WITHIN WESTERN LAW

The above list of differences within the Western law systems should not obscure the similarities, similarities that continue to increase. Many common-law countries have codified parts of their law; in the United States, for example, the Uniform Commercial Code has supplanted case law in most business matters. On the other hand, civil-law countries recognize that judges seeking to apply a particular section of the legal code will often look to see how other judges have handled similar cases. Civil-law countries have found ways of incorporating laypeople into the justice system. Some, such as Spain, have introduced juries into their systems while others, such as Germany, make use of lay judges who hear cases together with professional judges and together they decide both law and fact. Although admirers of the common law continue to praise the institution of the jury, the fact is that most cases are settled outside of the courtroom with the final agreement approved by a judge (Hayden 1987:263). The frequency of settlement reflects the expense and delay inherent in jury trials, as well as a reluctance to submit to the uncertainty of a jury verdict.

Finally, the most important thing that the two systems have in common is the belief that law is made by legislators and applied by judges. The laws may reflect religious values, but they are not the result of religious revelation. They may sometimes transform custom into law, but they may also recognize social, cultural, or technological change. They may reflect the power of a new interest group or the decline of an old one. They may change quickly and easily or as the result of a long and contentious process. In all of these circumstances, followers of Western law agree that law is a creation of human beings and therefore subject to change by human beings.

DISSATISFACTION WITH WESTERN LAW

In their purist forms, both forms of Western law solve disputes through processes that attempt to objectively weigh evidence and produce a verdict. The number of verdicts available is small—guilty or not guilty in a criminal case, for plaintiff or defendant in a civil case. In practice, most cases are settled before coming to trial and the results do not necessarily reflect these all-or-nothing outcomes. Reducing the criminal charges or accepting a plea to a lesser charge may reflect some uncertainty on the part of the state, while out-of-court settlements in civil cases usually involve some compromises from both parties. Even when cases do come to trial, the defendant may be found guilty on some charges but not on others. Likewise, the finders of fact in civil cases may find some fault with both parties by accepting a defense such as comparative negligence (finding that both parties were negligent, but not equally so) or by awarding little in the way of compensation. There is more flexibility in Western law than a casual study would indicate.

Nevertheless, past decades have found an increasing dissatisfaction with Western law's constraints. Particularly in common laws, victims in criminal cases are reduced to "complaining witnesses," and neither their material losses nor their emotional damages receive any attention. Although allowing the state to appropriate the role of victim (i.e., the government, not the victim, accuses the defendant in a criminal trial) has a number of advantages (e.g., the government has more resources than do most crime victims), it also means that the needs of the flesh-and-blood victim are often ignored. In civil cases, there is not a victim, per se, but one party may feel justified and the other aggrieved—feelings that are bound to increase rather than decrease their hostility toward each other.

The search for remedies to disputes has often led to other legal systems. Two of the most widely used of the borrowed mechanisms are mediation, originally modeled on techniques used in China, and restorative justice, inspired by the traditional legal systems of groups such as the Navajo Nation of the United States, Oji-Cree of Canada, and the Maori of New Zealand. While the institutions of all these cultures have been adapted to Western legal needs, all still clearly reveal their original inspirations.

In the People's Republic of China, mediators tend to be friends, neighbors, and relatives of the disputants. The mediators often identify the ideal outcome, and then work with the disputants to achieve it. They accept that the mediation process will take weeks, months, perhaps years. Western mediators, on the other hand, are sometimes volunteers, but they may also be trained in mediation techniques and paid for their services. They must be strangers to the disputants and are instructed not to determine an outcome but to support the disputants as they work out their own solution to their problem. The mediation process is brief; if an agreement is not reached within a number of hours, the meeting is brought to a close. While the Chinese and Western techniques are different, the aim is the same—to arrive at a resolution of the dispute that is satisfactory to both parties. Today, mediation in the United States is no longer an alternative to trial but is so much a part of the Western legal system that in many states courts will not hear certain cases unless the parties have tried mediation first.

Not all observers are enthusiastic over the movement to substitute mediation and negotiation for litigation. Laura Nader has been the most outspoken of a number of social scientists who believe that mediation and negotiation are a cut-rate form of justice that ignores inequalities between the parties and forces disputants to sacrifice their legal rights to an artificial goal of harmony. Nader (2002:121–123) outlines a theory of "harmony ideology" as pacification, a tool used by colonial powers to discourage forcible resistance from the people they colonized. She sees echoes of this in the attempt to convince disputants that their differences can be resolved by better communication rather than by a court of justice. She points out that where parties have a choice, the stronger party prefers mediation or arbitration, while the weaker party prefers a court of law (156–157).

If the mediation of disputes addresses itself to the civil side of Western law, restorative justice challenges the criminal side. Western criminal law is based on "retributive justice," the belief that justice is best served by punishing the offender. Advocates of "restorative justice" point out three failures of the Western criminal justice system. The first is the failure to meet the needs of the victim. Although European courts are able to combine civil and criminal cases, thereby allowing the victim to sue for damages, this process does not address the victim's nonmaterial needs. Common law does not do even this, seemingly assuming that the satisfaction of seeing offenders convicted and punished will satisfy the victims. Second, the high rate of recidivism indicates that the Western system also fails in deterring the offender from committing future crimes, and third, it does not successfully reintegrate the offender back into the community.

Attempts to remedy these failings took criminal justice reformers to societies practicing traditional law, societies whose aims and processes seemed to bring about the results that have escaped Western criminal justice. One observer of the restorative justice movement identifies its desired outcomes as follows:

- Offenders repair the harm resulting from their criminal acts;
- Offenders experience and express repentance for their misdeeds;
- Offenders are fully reintegrated into communities of law-abiding citizens; and
- Victims are healed of the trauma resulting from their experience (Johnstone 2003:4).

The emphasis, therefore, is on repairing the harm caused by the offenders rather than on punishing them. Equally important, restorative justice works to bring about a situation in which offenders are prepared to take responsibility as law-abiding members of a community, a community that is prepared to accept them in that role.

The Maori of New Zealand provide an example of restorative justice. A 17-year-old boy was accused of the attempted rape of a girl of 16. The boy admitted his guilt and the chief of the village convened a gathering. The victim came in first, accompanied by her parents and other relatives. Then the offender entered, together with members of his extended family. They sat on opposite sides of the meetinghouse. As soon as the boy pleaded guilty, the old women of the village began to berate him for breaking a sacred *tapu* in attacking a young woman, for bringing shame upon himself and his family. The boy and his relatives were reduced to tears.

At this point the penalty was announced. For the next 12 months, whenever there was a wedding or funeral service in the village, the boy's family would have to provide all the meat and vegetables. In addition, the boy had to paint the meetinghouse. Examination of the meetinghouse showed that the roofing iron had decayed, so the family had to replace it. After some time, because the meetinghouse belonged to everyone, the girl and her family helped prepare meals for the boy's family as they were working. Little by little, the unpleasant situation was reconciled, and together the two families repaired the dining room and surrounding fences. From start to finish, the process took about two years. Although the boy had been shamed before the entire village, he did not have a criminal record that would follow him for the rest of his life. The injury done to the girl was recognized and community support helped her to heal (Consedine 2003:153–154).

The processes used to bring about restorative justice vary, and its advocates caution against defining it in terms of means rather than ends. Nevertheless, certain elements appear with great regularity. These include:

- Victim–offender mediation, in which the victim explains the extent of the harm and victim and offender work out a means of restitution. This may include a form of community service in addition to direct reparation to the victim.

- Participation of the community, which means, at its simplest, that the mediator is a member of the community. More popular models include friends and relatives of both parties, who help find solutions and provide support to both victim and offender.

- An expression of regret and apology on the part of the offender.

- A plan formed by all of the participants to support the offender in his or her determination to avoid future misbehavior.

Whether it is really possible to adapt practices that are based on a possibly idealized model of traditional law into the Western legal system is still open to doubt. Nevertheless, an emerging body of research is beginning to demonstrate that restorative justice can be effective, even by the criteria of the Western criminal justice system (Bazemore 2005:131–148).

Chapter Five

Religious Law

Religious law is divine law, supposedly formulated by spiritual beings and meant to bring human behavior into harmony with spiritual dictates. Transgressions may be punished in the afterlife, but they should also be sanctioned by the living. This makes religious law different from religious mores, customs, or other rules. It assumes a community of believers willing to comply with the laws and willing to demand compliance from community members who do not. Where the community has the political status of a state, such as in Iran and Saudi Arabia, the laws of the state are based upon the laws of the religion. Some states enforce specific areas of religious law—most often family law, inheritance law, or land law—while basing the rest of their legal systems on secular sources.

God or gods reveal the laws to the religion's founders or prophets. The giving of the law is among the critical events of the religion's history and development. Willingness to abide by the laws of one's religion is in itself an act of worship. Religious law embodies the religion's moral code and its belief as to the proper relationship between humans and the supernatural and it also serves to define the community of believers. Obedience to the law Jehovah gave to Moses and the other prophets served to differentiate the Jews from the surrounding tribes, while obedience to the law that Allah gave to Muhammad distinguished Muslims from their polytheistic neighbors.

It is again necessary to confront the fact that the lines separating religious law from other types of law are not always clear. Some of Western law is based on Old Testament and New Testament teachings, and the law of continental European countries has often embodied the rules and procedures of the Roman Catholic Church. Whatever their source, these teachings became part of the civil law only when governments adopted them, applied them to all members of the population whether they were believers or not, and enforced them with the power of the state.

It is also true that many followers of customary law view it as being given by the gods. Navajos, for example, say that the Holy People taught law to the Navajo at the same time that they taught all the other aspects of Navajo culture, at the time of creation. Navajo law is certainly one of the things that make Navajos who they are. If a distinction must be made between customary and religious law, it has to be based on the fact that Navajo law has *always* been part of Navajo culture. It was given to the Navajos as a pillar of their way of life, not as a radical change in that way of life. It was given to the very first Navajos, not to a founder or prophet of a new religion. Law is not a component of Navajo religion; law and religion are simultaneous, integral components of Navajo culture.

Religious law presents its followers with a unique set of challenges. Because it is divine, it is eternal, universal, and perfect. However, in spite of being eternal, it exists in a world that is constantly changing. In spite of being universal, it was revealed to humans in a particular time and place and in particular historical circumstances. Because it is perfect, it cannot be altered or amended by mere human beings. Wrestling with these challenges is the story of religious law. Jewish and Islamic law provide examples.

JEWISH LAW

The word usually translated as "Jewish law" is *halakhah*, although a more literal translation would be "path." It is the path one follows to be an observant Jew. Although all parts of the halakhah have the status of law, it is actually made up of rules from several different sources.

The core of the halakhah are the 613 *mitzvot* (commandments) to be found in the Torah, the first five books of the Bible. These include very explicit rules, such as those found in the Ten Commandments given to the prophet Moses on Mount Sinai.

> Others are more implicit (the mitzvah to recite grace after
> meals, which is inferred from "and you will eat and be satisfied
> and bless the L-rd your G-D"), and some can only be ascertained
> by Talmudic[1] logic (that a man shall not commit incest with his
> daughter, which is derived from the commandment not to com-
> mit incest with his daughter's daughter).
>
> Some of the mitzvot overlap; for example, it is a positive com-
> mandment to rest on Shabbat (the Sabbath) and a negative
> commandment not to work on Shabbat. (Rich 2004)

Some of the mitzvot are so specific to time and place that they
simply cannot be observed in the here and now. Some of them relate
to proper behavior in the temple in Jerusalem, a structure that no
longer exists. Others relate to the state of Israel when it was ruled
by kings and had a government based on religious teachings. Since
there no longer is such a state, these mitzvot cannot be obeyed
today. Laws concerning agriculture pertain only to the state of
Israel, and others are to be obeyed only by certain descent groups.
There is great agreement that today there are 271 mitzvot that can
be observed by all Jews inside and outside Israel.[2]

While the mitzvot are said to come directly or indirectly from
God, other parts of the halakhah were posited by rabbis (distinguished scholars and teachers). The purpose of these laws (gezeirah) is to protect the mitzvot by making sure that they are not broken accidentally. For example, the mitzvah to abstain from work on
the Sabbath is protected by the gezeirah forbidding the handling of
tools or other implements of work. If you cannot touch such a tool,
you will not accidentally make use of it and break the command-
ment against working.

A third part of the halakhah consists of rabbinical rules not
derived from the Torah. *Takkanot* are meant to help the legal system adapt to political or social change or technological innovation
taking place after the time of the Torah. One example is the com-
mandment to light candles during the festival of Hanukkah, a festival that commemorates events that took place after the time of the
Torah. Other takkanot were fashioned during the medieval period
and pertained to the fact that Jews now lived surrounded by Christians. Some regulated commercial regulations, such as the one
demanding that no Jew act in bad faith toward a Christian. Others,
such as the one saying that Jews should not dress as Christians but
in a distinctive manner, were meant to keep Jews and Christians
apart. In more contemporary times, the Chief Rabbinate of Israel

has passed, among others, a takkanah specifying that neither men nor women may marry until they are 16 years of age.

The final source of Jewish law is *minhag* or custom. The word refers particularly to customs or religious practices that have no Biblical source but have been observed for so long that they "become as sacred and binding as laws instituted by the proper authorities" (*Jewish Encyclopedia* 2002). Jewish scholars recognize that many laws specified in the other sources are actually based on preexisting customs, but it is also true that some customs are based on other laws. For example, it was once a gezeirah to observe each of the religious holidays for two days rather than one. This was due to the fear that people outside of Israel might mistake the actual day of the holiday; doubling the days of observance reduced the odds that the holiday would be celebrated on the wrong day. This fear disappeared with the introduction of a nonlunar or mathematical calendar, but the suggestion that the second day be abolished was greeted with the reply that it was a custom that by now had been observed by so many generations that it should not be altered.

The total body of halakhah governs every aspect of Jewish life—food, clothing, marriage, property and property rights, crime and punishment, business practices, dealings with employees and servants, responsibilities toward the poor and unfortunate, time and conditions for prayers, and many more. Each law—regardless of its source—is equally binding. The main difference is that the punishment for breaking a mitzvah is more severe than that for not obeying other portions of the law. In addition, the mitzvot, having been given by God, cannot be altered by humans, while the gezeirah, takkanot, and minhag can, under very unusual circumstances, be modified by the rabbis.

ISLAMIC LAW

Like all religious law, Islamic law serves to distinguish its followers from nonbelievers and to remind believers of their religious identity. The history of Islamic law, however, began with an additional challenge—to weld a group of feuding Arabic tribes into a community of faith that would eventually cover the world. Today, well over a billion people representing every continent are Muslims and more than 50 countries identify themselves as being Islamic.

Jewish law was given to a small homogeneous tribe as a way of setting it apart from its neighbors. While Judaism has always accepted converts, it has never sought them. On the other hand, the aim of Muhammad, the founder and prophet of Islam, was to unite a hostile and culturally disparate people—ranging from desert nomad to farmer to urbane merchant—and then set out to convert the rest of the world and form it into a community of believers—the ummah.

Muhammad was born in the city of Mecca in approximately 570 CE to a respected but impoverished family. His parents died while he was young. He went into trade and gained such a reputation for honesty and ability that Kalidja, a wealthy merchant's widow, asked him first to handle her business, then to marry her. At the approximate age of 40, Muhammad had a vision of the Angel Gabriel, followed by voices proclaiming him (Muhammad) the Apostle of God. For the rest of his life, Muhammad would have visions during which he would hear and repeat the words of God, or Allah. His disciples collected and recorded what he said and these records became the Koran, the holy book of Islam and the first source of Islamic law. Almost as important is the *sunna*—the behavior, practices, and values of Muhammad, whose life serves as a model for all Muslims. Included in the sunna is the *hadith,* the collected sayings of Muhammad. Together, these comprise the *shariah,* the "path" that all Muslims should follow. A legal system based upon them is "shariah law." Other sources of Islamic law are *ijma,* or the consensus of the Islamic community; *qiyas,* or reasoning by analogy from the other sources; and *ijtihad,* independent reasoning.

The first century after Muhammad's death in 632 saw the establishment of four great schools (*madhhabs*) of Islamic jurisprudence. Each was named for the imam, or local religious leader, whose work is the school's foundation. Although they differ slightly in certain areas—inheritance and the rules of private and public worship, among others—each is acceptable to the majority Sunni branch of Islam. The Shia branch, found primarily in India and the lands that formerly comprised Persia, adheres to a fifth school. The learned analyses of the founding imams so impressed their followers that they felt that the imams had closed all gaps in the law and that from then on, ijtihad would no longer be allowed.[3] Closing this source of change has made it more difficult, although by no means impossible, for Islamic law to deal with a changing world (Nasr 2003:77–80).

In ways similar to those of Jewish law, Islamic law penetrates all areas of the believer's life—dress, food, sanitation, times for prayer, and days of rest. But it also reflects Islam's call to reform— a call to a moral life that begins with recognition of the unity and power of Allah and continues with complete submission to divine will. Shariah introduced a new category of crimes and punishments, crimes not recognized by the pre-Islamic societies. These *hadd* crimes include adultery, fornication, false accusation of adultery, apostasy, consumption of alcohol, and theft and highway robbery. The punishments for these crimes are stipulated in the Koran and cannot be altered by human judges, since they are crimes against God, and not against other human beings or society.

The punishments are capital or corporal, but trials are surrounded by extensive substantive and procedural safeguards for the accused that make conviction difficult. The law says, for example, that it is impossible to steal anything that could be unowned; this includes wood, grass, fish and birds, fruits that have not been harvested, and meat that is easily perishable. Things that *should* not be owned, such as alcohol and musical instruments, cannot be the objects of theft, nor can holy books. A person cannot steal anything of which he or she is part owner, such as public property. Theft must be by stealth, so open robbery is not included. Theft involves only objects of which the accused has no right of custody, so one is not guilty of removing an object from the house of a near relative or from a place that the thief had permission to enter. Finally, theft involves removal, so a person caught red-handed with an object within premises where the object belongs is not guilty of theft (Barton, et al. 1983:427).

There are also procedural safeguards. In the absence of a confession, the testimony of two male Muslim witnesses is required. These witnesses must be of good character, and the judge takes great care to inquire into their background, reputation, place of origin, and relationship to the parties to the case.

Another set of safeguards involves presumptions. When the sides present conflicting proof, the judge chooses one side over the other based on presumptions that have become judicially recognized.

> He will, for example, regard those who live nearby as more likely than those who live farther away to know if a husband has indeed been mistreating his wife, to give the subsequent testimony of witnesses to a land transaction less weight than a

notarized document made out at the time, or to regard as more
credible those who claim actually to have seen a marriage cele-
bration take place than those who simply heard about the
event. Cultural assumptions, molded and articulated by judicial
action, deeply suffuse the content and application of the court's
assessment of facts. (Rosen 1989:28)

Rosen notes the similarity of the assumptions by which courts act
and by which ordinary people act in everyday life.

A final safeguard is the decisive oath. If the plaintiff or prosecu-
tor cannot prove his or her case satisfactorily, the defendant may be
asked to take an oath of innocence. If he or she does so, that ends
the case and the plaintiff may be punished for false accusation.
Some of the schools of law allow the defendant to decline the oath
and ask that the plaintiff take it instead. Again, the taking of the
oath settles the case.

Although the hadd crimes and their punishments were new and
designed to bring people closer to the Muslim ideal of proper behavior, Islamic law also recognized older categories of punishment.
Qisas means "retaliation." It refers to killings and to woundings
that do not prove fatal. The victim or the victim's heirs have the
right to kill the offender under the supervision of a judge. If they do
not demand qisas, they are entitled to *dyia,* monetary compensation. Finally, there is *ta'zir,* meaning "to censure or repel." These
punishments were added to Islamic law some time after the death
of Muhammad and are intended to reform the offender. Judges have
wide discretion in this category, which ranges from discreet repri-
mand to imprisonment, whipping, and banishment.

Although criminal law often receives the most attention, it comprises only one small part of the body of laws designed to unify and
improve the Islamic community. Muslims themselves take particular pride in their inheritance law, which is designed to bring about
a number of Muhammad's goals. In the pre-Islamic period, the most
important social unit was the tribe—patrilineal and patriarchal.
Loyalty to the tribe was a cardinal virtue and intertribal battles
were common. Consistent with this was the pattern of inheritance
that specified that a decedent's property went first to his male
(agnatic) descendants, then to his male ascendants, always to a
closer rather than a more distant male relative, and preferably to
someone related through both parents. Muhammad's reforms
strengthened the nuclear family at the expense of the tribe and also

strengthened the position of women; the Koran established rights of inheritance between husband and wife and in favor of certain female relatives such as mothers, daughters, and sisters. Most schools of law see these newer rights as being superimposed upon the old agnatic rules rather than supplanting them. Reconciling these two sets of rules has presented some of the greatest challenges to Islamic legal scholars.

Even though the new Koranic inheritance rules gave females some rights, males received twice as much as females. It is important to remember, however, that European law at the time and for centuries to come gave women even far fewer rights of inheritance or control of property that their Islamic counterparts. The Prophet did other things to raise the status of women. While the pre-Islamic law allowed men to take as many wives as they liked and was silent on how wives should be treated, Muhammad allowed only four wives and, most important, said all wives must be treated equally in every way. Islamic law also gave women some rights of divorce as well as of support for and custody of minor children. Although women could only testify in some types of court cases and their testimony was worth only half as much as that of a man, the pre-Islamic situation gave no credibility whatsoever to women's words.

Saudi Arabia and Iran are among the relatively few Islamic countries that have adopted shariah law as their exclusive law. Others, such as Egypt, use it for selected areas of law, such as family and land law. Morocco offers a choice of law in a number of areas. Whether or not the law is being enforced, however, does not change the fact that all Muslims are responsible for their actions before God (Rosen 1984) and the law provides guidance for actions.

Due to the effects of colonialism, illiteracy, poverty, and isolation, some communities that think they are applying Islamic law are actually misinterpreting it. "Colonial rule paralyzed Muslim societies, congealed thought and froze their histories. . . . It was easy to fall back to old, pre- or non-Islamic, superstitions and beliefs" (Ahmed 1988:117). For example, Muslim practitioners of female circumcision often defend it as being commanded by Islam. In fact, neither the Koran nor any other source of Islamic law mentions the practice. Ahmad points out that, in fact, women are permitted to seek a divorce if their husbands do not provide them with sexual satisfaction. He deduces from this that Islamic law prohibits anything (e.g., circumcision) that would tend to diminish women's sexual pleasure. Female circumcision is a custom that probably originated in pre-Islamic times (Ahmad 2004).

FUNCTIONS OF RELIGIOUS LAW

It is possible to find—or at least speculate about—rationales for some religious laws. For example, Hindu law states that cows are sacred and may not be eaten. The admonition not to eat cows may have originated in secular practicality, since cows may be more valuable to India as producers of fertilizer and bullocks (the common draft animals) than they would be as beef. Pigs may be a cheap form of food for sedentary agricultural communities, because pigs consume vegetable scraps, but an impractical luxury for nomadic groups, such as early Jews and Muslims (Harris 1974:11–57.) There are, however, two readily apparent functions of all religious law.

The first is to remind believers of their beliefs and their religious identity by constantly turning ordinary daily acts into acts of religious observance. Obeying the law while rising, dressing, eating, and working make believers feel that they are living their lives in a spiritual manner. The second, and closely related, is the fact that religious law brings believers together while it separates them from nonbelievers. It is easy to obey dietary laws when nearby butchers, grocery stores, restaurants, as well as potential hosts and guests, are obeying the same laws. Living in a community of nonbelievers makes obeying these laws far more difficult. It is easy to conduct business according to religious law and take disputes to religious courts if all parties are members of the same faith; it may be impossible if they are not. Stopping all activities because it is time for prayer is perceived as normal when all participants are of the same faith; it may be perceived as peculiar or alien when they are not. Closing your shop on the Sabbath presents no problems when all of your customers also observe the Sabbath on the same day, but it is a major obstacle to profit if that is a day on which your customers love to shop.

Another way in which religious law creates an identity for the community of believers is to outlaw practices common among nearby nonbelievers. For example, the laws given to both Moses and Muhammad prohibited their followers from making idols. This clearly distinguished them from surrounding polytheists (e.g.,

Babylonians) whose idols were a focus for worship and sacrifice. The idea of a day of rest was also unknown, let alone that servants and slaves should also have such a day. Islamic prohibition of drinking and gambling set Muslims apart from the neighboring tribes that indulged heavily in these activities. Islamic inheritance laws recognizing women as heirs served a similar function.

RELIGIOUS LAW AND CHANGE

But how does religious law meet its special challenge of applying law revealed in a particular time and place and under particular circumstances to a world that is diverse and always changing? Jewish and Islamic law both provide good examples.

Jewish law was originally given to a patriarchal tribe living just north of the Arabian Peninsula, a monotheistic nomadic group depending on its herds of sheep and goats. Surrounding it were similar groups of nomads, polytheistic and worshipping idols. First the Israelites needed to distinguish themselves from their neighbors. But the Israelites were on their way to becoming settled and building a state, and their laws also needed to reflect that.

With the coronation of Saul in 1020 BCE, the Jews had established the formidable kingdom of Israel, with a body of laws that regulated their relationship to God, to the state, and to each other. Two independent nations, Israel and Judah, were created and lasted until they were conquered respectively by the Assyrians in 721 BCE and the Babylonians in 587 BCE. Returning from exile the Jewish people lived in the land that had formerly been their kingdom and followed many of their laws and customs, even after they became a part of the Roman Empire. This situation came to an abrupt end in 74 CE, when Rome responded to a Jewish revolt by destroying the main temple in Jerusalem and forcing the Jewish residents to leave the area.

This was the beginning of the Jewish Diaspora. Jews were scattered into many countries in different parts of the world, countries with different climates, economies, governments, and cultures. In a few of these places Jews were welcomed, in others they were tolerated, in still others they lived under constant threat. Jews were no longer pastoral nomads and most were not even agriculturalists; instead, they were traders, manufacturers, artisans, scholars, and professionals. Although their communities had varying degrees of autonomy, they were no longer the rulers of a state. They lived through centuries of political and technological change. They needed law that would recognize this situation, but they also needed to recognize the divine origin of Jewish law.

There are a number of precedents and sources for change in Jewish law. One has already been mentioned, and that is the fact that many of the mitzvot, the rules to be found in the Torah, are relevant only to specific circumstances or persons. Another, also already mentioned, is the recognition that rabbis always could make changes or reinterpret gezeirah, takkanot, or minhag, should they deem it necessary.

Judaism does not have a hierarchical structure. There is no one person or body to interpret law for all Jews. Instead, law has been interpreted and applied over time by sages and rabbis—scholars recognized and respected for their learning and wisdom, but who have no special authority and who have often disagreed with each other. Related to the lack of hierarchy is the acknowledgement of local differences and local demands. "Everything depends on the custom of the land" was often repeated by rabbis deciding civil cases (*Jewish Encyclopedia* 2002). For example, it was a matter of law that two people who agreed to divide a piece of land had to contribute equally to the building of a fence between the two parcels, but the nature of the building material and the dimensions of the fence were to be decided by local custom. If someone hired a laborer for a day, local custom dictated exactly how long the day was to be. Whether or not a servant had to pay for broken tools or utensils depended on the custom of the place. Custom also decided whether certain rabbinical pronouncements were to be obeyed.

> For example, around the year 1000 CE, a Rabbenu Gershom Me'or Ha-Golah instituted a takkanah prohibiting polygyny, a practice clearly permitted by the Torah and the Talmud. It was accepted by Askenazic Jews, who lived in Christian countries where polygyny was not permitted, but was not accepted by Sephardic Jews, who lived in Islamic countries where men were permitted up to four wives. (Rich 2004)

Jewish law also has had to deal with technological developments. Tay-Sachs is a genetic condition that appears disproportionately among Jews. A Tay-Sachs baby will suffer from dementia, blindness, paralysis, and an early death. It is carried on a recessive gene; this means that if two people carrying the gene marry, the odds are that one out of four of their children will have the disease. Rabbis have dealt with this situation in a number of different ways. Because marriage between close relatives increases the odds of a Tay-Sachs child, some rabbis forbid marriage between first cousins and between uncles and nieces, although such marriages took place in the Bible. On the other hand, because marriage between relatives does not actually cause the disease but just increases the chances, other rabbis, mindful of the Biblical precedents, refuse to ban them. And still others strongly caution against marriage between close relatives. Now, however, it is possible to screen prospective parents to see if they carry the gene. If one or neither has the recessive gene, guaranteeing that their children will not have the disease, should they be allowed to marry even if they are first cousins? If both carry the gene, should the marriage be forbidden even if they are not related? Should screening be mandatory? Up to now, there is no consensus on these matters.

The absence of a single hierarchy also allows Jews to choose for themselves the role that Jewish law plays in their lives. North American Jews have divided into several groups. Among them, orthodox Jews believe that Mosaic law as found in the Torah and interpreted in the Talmud is applicable and binding upon Jews no matter where or when they live. Conservative Jews also find that Jewish law is binding, but think that it may be interpreted and adapted to fit modern circumstances. Reform Jews represent a nineteenth-century movement seeking to reconcile historical Judaism with modern life. Reform Judaism requires adhering to the faith and philosophy of Judaism rather than to ritual and religious law. For example, orthodox Jews obey all the dietary laws found in the Torah. These include lists of forbidden foods, as well as strictures on the production, preparation, and serving of all food products. Obviously, it is easiest to obey such laws when one lives and works in a community where approved foods are easily available and where one's friends and coworkers are observing the same rules. Conservative Jews, whose lives often take them outside of the Jewish community, may obey the same rules, but often confine themselves to avoiding the forbidden foods, such as pork and shellfish. Reform Jews most often find dietary laws to be irrelevant to their attempts to observe the faith and ethics of Judaism in the contemporary world.

Followers of Islamic law have also found ways of adapting to change. Although the end of ijtihad reduced the flexibility of Islamic law, it did not end it. When the Ottoman Empire decided to codify shariah law, it included opinions from all four Sunni schools of law, selecting in each case the reading that best suited its intended reforms (Anderson 1957:26). Over time, many jurists have found it possible to be faithful to the law's intent while adapting to modern circumstances. For example, because trade was an important part of Arabic culture, much of Koranic law deals with commercial matters. The underlying philosophy is one of fairness and honest dealing, of avoiding unjust enrichment. One of the best-known laws in this area is the one forbidding borrowing or lending money at interest because it produces profit at another's expense.

This prohibition makes it impossible for a Muslim to take out a conventional home mortgage since mortgages involve repaying the loan with interest. Islamic scholars have devised ways in which someone unable to buy a home for cash can nevertheless acquire a home and still obey both the letter and the spirit of the law. One of these is a declining balance co-ownership, in which the would-be homeowner and a professional investment company buy the home as partners. The homeowner lives in the house and pays his partner an amount each month as rent. He also pays another amount in order to increase his share of the equity. As his equity increases, his monthly rent decreases until he is the sole owner. Another possibility is leasing to own, with the investment company buying the house and leasing it back to the homeowner (Morris, Thomas, and DeLorenzo 2002).

There are many cases of dispute or disagreement in which Islamic law does not provide a set of abstract rules that must be uniformly applied. Instead, judges refer to a set of ethical principles, dealing with each case on an individual basis. This type of justice "partakes of regularities which reveal not only Islamic legal history, but also the interplay between Islamic law and the society in which it is rooted" (Rosen 1980:217). Islamic justice reflects the time and place in which it is applied.

These are just some examples of the ways in which the seemingly unalterable laws of religion can accommodate changing circumstances and practices.

Notes

[1] The Talmud consists of commentaries on the Torah and comprises the authoritive body of Jewish tradition.

[2] The legal system of modern Israel is based on Western law and resembles the civil law tradition in relying on legal codes rather than case law. There are religious courts for Jews, Christians, and Druze, which are restricted to matters of marriage and divorce. Similar courts for Muslims handle all personal status matters.

[3] Although some scholars see *ijtihad* as functioning into the Middle Ages and a few feel that it was never actually forbidden (Hallaq 1984: 3–41).

Chapter Six

Traditional or
Customary Law

Traditional or customary law is based on *custom and tradition.*

The sentence above, although true, is ineffective in distinguishing customary[1] law from other families of law. All types of Western law incorporate tradition; common law in particular is very explicit about this. Western law judges today often decide commercial cases according to "the custom and usage of the industry." On the other hand, some societies using customary law believe that those customs were given to them by gods or spiritual beings, making their customary law similar to religious law. Finding the rather blurry lines that allow us to speak of "traditional" or "customary" law calls for a more careful investigation.

SOCIETIES WHERE CUSTOMARY LAW IS FOUND

We can begin by looking at the types of societies in which we find customary law. First, they tend to be rather small, making it possible for people to know each other on a face-to-face basis. Kinship is an important—perhaps the most important—organizing principle, with lineages, clans, and moieties[2] dominating social structure. Ascription plays a larger role than achievement. This is a way of saying that gender, age, birth order, and the status of parents are more important in determining the course of one's life than are talent, ability, or luck. Rights and obligations are more a result of a person's place in society, and less a result of contracts or other voluntary undertakings.

Societies with customary law also have certain types of economies. Most often we find such law in hunting and gathering and horticultural societies or in pastoral ones (societies that live off of herds of sheep, goats, or cattle). Some agricultural societies rely exclusively on customary law, but industrial societies, although they sometimes use tradition as a basis for law, never rely exclusively on it.

Finally, customary law is found in societies that are *relatively* homogeneous. This means that the members of a society have much in common and tend to share the same history, religion, values, and beliefs. The word "relatively" matters here; a society in which all members share all of these things has probably never existed. We are simply looking at groups that have *more* in common than the diverse, stratified, multiethnic, multicultural groups we find in major agricultural, industrial, or postindustrial societies.

CHARACTERISTICS OF CUSTOMARY LAW

The legal systems developed by societies that rely on customary law may differ greatly from each other, but certain traits can be found in most of them.

Groups that practice traditional law think of their law as being as old as the group itself. "It is the way we have always done it" is one common answer to a question about the origin of traditional law. "It has been the law since time immemorial" (Perry 1996). Where a people do have a narrative of their law's origin, it usually coincides with the origin of the people themselves. The Holy People gave law to the Navajo just as they bestowed upon them all the other elements of Navajo culture. Natives of the American Pueblos of the Southwest, who believe that their ancestors climbed from the earth's core to its crust, say that their laws "came up with us."

Traditional law is localized. The people who subscribe to a particular form of traditional law feel that it is the proper form of law for *them*, for a certain people living in a certain place. They may speak of "the Navajo way" or *mekgwa le melao ya Setswana,* "Tswana custom and law" (Gulbrandsen 1996:126). While followers of Western law and of many forms of religious law may attempt to convert others to their form of law through colonialism or conquest, followers of traditional law see their law as an integral part of their culture and therefore not necessarily appropriate for those of another culture. In other words, traditional law is *indigenous.* This means there are many different examples of traditional law, since each society devises its own, rather than borrowing from another society or having another group's form of traditional law imposed upon it.

Procedure in traditional law does not revolve around technicalities. There are no legal specialists—no full-time legislators, judges, lawyers, or clerks. To the extent that these roles exist at all, they are filled by people chosen for their age, wisdom, knowledge of the culture, neutrality, political post, or kinship position. In some societies there was no third party at all; the disputants and their supporters were expected to work out an acceptable solution. Philip Gulliver (1969:26) reports for the Arusha of northern Tanzania, "Each disputant recruits a body of supporters, and the two parties meet in peaceful assembly to discuss the matter and to negotiate an agreed settlement."

Since we usually find traditional law in nonliterate societies, it will come as no surprise that traditional law is unwritten. It is part of the culture's oral tradition and children learn it in the same way as they learn any other part of the culture. It is more likely to be expressed as norms, values, and customs, as a code of proper behavior under certain circumstances, than as an abstract set of rules. Today, we do find traditional law in written form. In some societies this is because the anthropologists who studied them included law in their ethnographies. Often, as members of the society became literate in other languages, they wrote down their society's laws. Finally, many societies that previously had only a spoken language subsequently developed writing and committed their legal system to paper. Of course, the very act of writing down what had previously been conveyed orally changed its nature; it could transform what had been a code easily adapted to specific situations to an abstract, inflexible set of rules (Merry 1992:365.) But this was not inevitable—although many Tswana appreciated Ian Schepera's recording of their law in *Handbook of Tswana Law and Custom*, they never made use of it in litigation or court proceedings (Gulbrandsen 1996:143). In practice, Tswana law remains an oral code, not a rigid set of rules.

Although traditional law is rooted in custom and tradition, it is not the same as custom and tradition. First, not all custom is law; only some customs meet the legal test of being backed by force sanctioned by society. Second, traditional law resembles other types of law in that it is constantly being interpreted as it is applied to changing times and novel situations. Hoebel (1954) gives a classic example from the Cheyenne.

> Wolf Lies Down returned to his camp to find that a friend had taken his horse without asking permission. When after a while the friend had not returned with the horse, Wolf Lies Down put his case before the four elected chiefs of the Elk Soldiers, the military society to which he belonged. The chiefs sent out a messenger to find the friend and bring him home. When he returned, the friend explained that he had meant only to borrow the horse, that he intended to return it, that he would make generous restitution for any loss that the horse's owner might have incurred, and he made Wolf Lies Down his blood brother. This restitution and reconciliation ended this particular case, but the Elk Soldier Chiefs clearly saw that such disputes might not be settled so amicably in the future and decided to head off potential problems. In addition to resolving this particular case, they also made a new law. "Now we shall make a new rule. There shall be no more borrowing of horses without asking. If any man takes another's goods without asking, we shall go over and get them back for him. More than that, if the taker tries to keep them, we will give him a whipping." (24)

Customary law can also change in order to preserve traditional values in the face of new challenges (Gulbrandsen 1996). The customary law of the Tswana of the British Protectorate of Bechuanaland (now Botswana) held that the earnings of unmarried sons belonged to their father, who used the money to add to the family's herd of cattle. In the early 1900s, as single young men migrated to cities for wage-paying jobs, at least one Tswana kingdom changed the law so that migrant sons might use their earnings to buy their own cattle. While this might appear as an instance of the law recognizing the diminished influence of the family and the growing power of individualism, the Tswana didn't see it that way.

> The reason why we insisted that migrant workers should be
> entitled to the cattle they had bought with their wages, rather
> than their being included in the father's herd, was that the
> fathers used to take the money brought home by their sons, so
> the young men started to spend their earnings on girls and
> other useless things before they went home. This was a very
> destructive situation, which had to be corrected by law. (146)

The new law enforced the old values, the values that said that
income should be invested in cattle, not spent on foolish things—no
matter whether it was fathers or sons who did the spending.

Tswana political leaders had the right to make new laws, but
they couldn't do it arbitrarily. Extensive consultation with council-
ors and headman had to take place, and a new law was proclaimed
only after extensive public debate. In addition, the Tswana believed
that the lawmakers communicated with the ancestors on important
issues, perhaps though dreams. If the people did not like new legislation, they might blame it on poor communication with the ancestors (Gulbrandsen 1996:144).

UNDERLYING ASSUMPTIONS AND VALUES

Traditional law rests on assumptions and values that are not
absent from other forms of law but are more pronounced in the
small, kin-based, nonindustrial societies being considered here.
One such assumption is that the rights and well-being of the group
are more important than those of the individual. Another assumption is that reconciliation and restitution are more important than
punishment and retribution. This is particularly important when
the disputants are close neighbors or kin, but somewhat less so if
one or both of the parties are strangers or outsiders. Traditional
legal procedures do not necessarily find for one party or the other;
instead, the preferred outcome may be some type of compromise,
one that will allow members of a small society to live and work
together in the future. Friends and relatives will encourage the disputants to accept the verdict.

This certainly does not mean that all traditional legal procedures actually achieve reconciliation and restitution. Gulliver (1969)
gives an example from the Ndendeuli of southern Tanzania. A dispute over bridewealth was mediated to the apparent satisfaction of

both parties, and the mediation concluded with all concerned partaking of beer provided by the mediator. However, Zadiki, a prominent kinsman of one of the disputants and a cousin of the mediator, felt that the mediator had behaved with bias. Relations between these two men were already frosty and the mediation made them worse. In a later case, the two men were members of opposing parties; ordinarily, two such cousins would have joined together as mediators in the dispute. Although the dispute was resolved in ways that allowed a working relationship to continue, neither the immediate nor the long-term roots of the cousins' bad relationship were resolved. Their hostility continued to reverberate through further disputes (35–56.) The pressure to arrive at a settlement may make disputants feel that their individual desires for justice have been sacrificed to the group's need to be able to live and work together.

Traditional societies are more likely to see wrongdoing as bad behavior that should be corrected rather than as the act of a bad person who should be punished. The Sandy Lake First Nation of Ontario puts it like this. "The Indian communities view a wrongdoing as a misbehavior which requires teaching or an illness which requires healing" (Ross 2003:125).

Much of Western legal procedure consists of narrowing the questions to be presented to the court; good lawyers develop skill in isolating "the issue" to be decided from its background. Fans of televised Western courtroom drama become familiar with the objection "incompetent, irrelevant, and immaterial!" and they learn that this objection is frequently sustained. Customary law is also concerned with "the issue," but in addition, it tends to be interested in the context surrounding the issue—the history, personalities, and moral issues involved. "Relevance" is broadly defined, perhaps to include the entire record of the relationships between the disputants, a record that may well include that of their ancestors for many generations. The issue in dispute is not considered in isolation, but is seen as one event in a chain of events that stretches into the past and will stretch into the future.

Most of the time, traditional legal systems settle cases by applying wisdom, common sense, a sense of justice, and the culture's rules to the facts as presented by the parties, witnesses, and anyone else who is seen as having something to contribute. At other times, however, traditional systems make use of *oaths* or *ordeals*, decision-making techniques that invoke the help of nature or the supernatural. Once more, the line between customary and religious law blurs. In customary law, oaths involve swearing that one is telling the truth, knowing that a lie will invoke divine sanctions that may last for generations. While oaths are found most often in customary law, they share similarities with the decisive oath of innocence of Islamic law. Western common law also makes use of oaths, asking witnesses to swear on a holy book that that they will tell only the truth in the courtroom proceeding. While the primary function of these contemporary Western oaths is to emphasize the solemnity of the court and the very secular penalties attached to perjury, in appearance and probably in history they greatly resemble the oath found in traditional law.

Ordeals involve asking—or forcing—the accused to submit to a dangerous test, believing that an innocent person will survive or feel no pain. The Loma people of Nigeria provide an example of the ordeal as a method of deciding guilt or innocence. A diviner heats a pot of palm oil until it is smoking and drops a brass ring into it. He smears the arm of the accused with a paste made of leaves and repeats what everybody knows—that if the accused is innocent, the oil will not hurt him, but if the person is guilty the oil will burn him and cause pain and blisters. The accused has the right to reject the ordeal and plead guilty. If he agrees to go through with it, he plunges his arm into the pot of smoking oil and retrieves the ring and then displays his arm to the assembled villagers. If pain prevents him from grasping the ring or if his arm is burnt and blistered, he is guilty and liable to be punished. If he shows no signs of pain and his arm remains uninjured, he is considered innocent.

Other types of ordeals involve grabbing bars of hot iron, having heated knives rubbed across one's back, or walking on hot coals. Although skeptics point out ways in which ordeals can be rigged—and both believers and anthropologists agree that this has happened—there are also objective observers who have found ordeals to be convincing. One possible explanation is that the guilty feel anxiety that expresses itself physically; for example, a guilty person may be hesitant to reach into the pot of hot oil, with the result being that his skin is in contact with the oil for a longer period than that of the innocent person, who approaches the oil quickly and confidently. The theory is that the ordeal works in much the same way as the polygraph machine, which measures the physiological effects produced by guilt.

Finally, traditional law often sees the settlement of a dispute as an occasion to teach the culture's norms and values. Even litigants who are found to be in the right may be scolded for bad behavior, while judgments frequently are reminiscent of sermons. In cultures where the wrongdoer is perceived as being disturbed rather than wicked—such as the Navajo—the community-wide efforts made to bring the offender back into harmony are themselves cited as examples of the community's cooperation and willingness to work together for the common good.

Many of these points can be clarified by examining a case Max Gluckman (1955) reported from the Barotse of Rhodesia, which today is the nation of Zimbabwe. Even though the case occurred in 1942, it demonstrates a number of traits common to traditional law. A complaint would be brought to the *kuta*. Gluckman points out the kuta is not a body specialized in law but is the council, the general governing body, with administrative and legislative functions as well as judicial ones. Some of its members hold their seats due to their hereditary positions while others are appointed. After all evidence is heard, each member of the kuta renders his own verdict; the last person to speak—the most senior member—sums up the sense of the group and the result is referred to the king, who may confirm it, reject it, alter it, or send it back to the kuta for further deliberation.

In the case being used as an example, three brothers sued their father's elder brother, the village headman, over some gardens. The headman had actually raised the brothers after their own father died. The brothers had been living outside of the village and the rule—acknowledged by all—was that if people moved away from their village, they lost their gardens. The case should, therefore, have been a simple one since no one disputed that the brothers were not living in the village.

But the litigants did not confine themselves to "the issue," and the court did not expect them to. The right to cultivate the gardens was embedded in the history of the relationships among the parties and the moral standing of all concerned. The brothers began by stating their grievance and the events leading up to it. They testified that the uncle's son had committed adultery with the wife of one of the brothers. The adulterer did not pay the required fine and when the aggrieved husband complained, the headman drove the betrayed husband out of the village. The headman also suggested very strongly that the other brothers leave. He and his son then started cultivating the brothers' gardens. The brothers stated that they would like to return to the village, but were unable to, due to the hostility of the headman.

When the brothers finished explaining their case to the kuta, it was the turn of the defendants. The headman's son alleged that some time ago one of the brothers had cuckolded the headman's sister's son. He claimed that the brothers had fled the village rather than being driven out and he complained of a long series of acts that indicated that the brothers were not respectful of their family obligations. He felt that the brothers did not wish to return to the village, but wanted to work their gardens while living elsewhere. The brothers retorted that the headman had favored his own son's interests over theirs and that he had ignored opportunities to reconcile the members of the family. The proceeding became a recital of grievances in which each litigant professed that he was a moral person who exemplified the norms of the culture while the opponents were stingy, selfish, and indifferent to the values of the society.

Members of the audience then gave their own testimony, confirming or denying the words of the litigants, and contributing any information they might consider relevant. This information might bear directly upon the matter of the gardens, but it might just as well pertain to the history of the family members and to incidents having no immediate connection to the garden dispute. These witnesses did not hesitate to give their own opinion concerning the respective moral standing of the parties and of the proper outcome of the case. Members of the kuta listened patiently and attentively to all of this, asking questions and requesting additional information.

Finally, each member of the kuta gave his assessment of the situation. There was no disagreement over the law—only persons living in the village could cultivate village gardens. But no member saw this as the only matter for the court. Instead, all of the parties to the case were reproached for harboring grievances and failing to reconcile. The brothers received the majority of the blame for behaving badly to the headman, the brother of their father, the man who had raised them. Also in for his share of blame was a village official who had told the brothers that if the headman told them to leave, they must leave. The kuta felt that his first duty was to bring about a reconciliation. The right to cultivate the fields became a secondary matter as the kuta went about what it saw as its most important responsibility—healing a breach in village and kin relationships and maintaining civic order and solidarity. The members all agreed on the final judgment—the brothers should return to the village and be warmly greeted by the headman and his son. They should live in the village and work their gardens, always aware that their uncle had the right to take the gardens when they left. Any further disrespect by the brothers would be dealt with firmly by the court. Gluckman reports that he heard nine years later that all the family members were living in amity.

CUSTOMARY LAW TODAY

The forgoing pages describe characteristics of customary law and the societies that use it. Today, societies such as these no longer exist independently but are inevitably incorporated into nation-states. They have become literate and may have members who are highly educated. They interact with people outside of the group and often have members who live part-time in cities. Their economies have become more complex and may depend at least indirectly on foreign trade and multinational corporations. They have been subjected to imperialism and colonialism. For any or all of these reasons, traditional legal systems today operate in limited circumstances, restricted in the types of cases they may try, the persons whose complaints they may hear, and/or the right of appeal.

At the time that Gluckman was reporting the case described above, Barotseland was part of a British Protectorate. Although the Barotse had an established hierarchy of courts for at least two centuries, the British altered the existing system and radically curtailed its jurisdiction and powers. The British deprived the traditional courts of the power to try cases of murder, witchcraft, and any case that involved a nonnative, either as a party or as a witness. The courts were also forbidden to inflict certain traditional penalties, including death, throttling, and unlimited flogging, although they gained the formerly unknown penalty of imprisonment. Perhaps most important is the fact that reports of all criminal cases had to be submitted to officers of the British colonial government and that any case could ultimately be appealed to a colonial court. Finally, a colonial government official could sit as an "advisor" in any traditional court.

The United States provides a different example of traditional law and the results of its clash with Western law. As the white population expanded westward it encountered tribes of Native Americans, encounters that often resulted in armed conflict. A frequent result of these hostilities was a treaty in which the Indians would be confined to a limited area of land but on that land they would be recognized as sovereign nations, free to govern themselves and apply their own law. That is how things stood on an afternoon in August 1881, on the Great Sioux Reservation in Dakota Territory, when Crow Dog shot and killed Chief Spotted Tail. Crow Dog was arrested and imprisoned in a cell in Fort Niobara, Nebraska. While Crow Dog was in jail, the families of the two men met and, following tribal law and extensive negotiation, Crow Dog's family provided restitution to the family of the victim, namely, $600 in cash, eight horses, and a blanket. As far as the Sioux were concerned, the aims of restitution and reconciliation were accomplished and the case was settled.

Spotted Tail's white friends on and around the reservation saw it differently. Spotted Tail was regarded as a "progressive" chief, one who was ready to lead his people into white ways and modern times. His popularity made it difficult for his non-Indian friends to accept that cash, horses, and a blanket would allow his murderer to go free; as far as they were concerned, Spotted Tail's death was unavenged and his assassin unpunished. They wanted justice—justice in Western terms.

Ignoring the fact that the case had already been settled according to Sioux traditional law, the territorial government of Dakota tried Crow Dog in the town of Deadwood, found him guilty, and sentenced him to death. Crow Dog's lawyers appealed to the United States Supreme Court, which found that the United States and, thus, the Territory of Dakota, had no right to try Crow Dog because Indian tribes were inherently sovereign and that part of that sovereignty was the right to administer their own law (*Ex Parte Crow Dog*, 109 U.S.556 [1883]). Crow Dog was set free, returned to the reservation, continued to resist the United States government, and died in his late 70s (Harring 1994).

But the Supreme Court did not stop there. It pointed out that Congress had the power to reduce or even extinguish tribal sovereignty. The fact that it had not done so in the case of criminal law meant that the Sioux retained the right to apply their own law to their own people on their own reservation. The Court could not have sent a clearer message. In 1885, Congress passed the Major Crimes Act, which stated that the federal government had jurisdiction over seven felonies—murder, manslaughter, rape, assault with intent to kill, arson, burglary, and larceny—committed on Indian land. By confining traditional law to civil cases and minor crimes (distinctions not made in traditional Indian law) Congress undermined the ability of the Indians to govern themselves.

The debates leading up to the passage of the act make clear that the lawmakers considered Indian law inferior to Western law and that the imposition of Western law was to be a step in "civilizing" the Indians. Just as the British doubted the ability of the Tswana or Barotse to handle their legal affairs without European supervision, so Euro-Americans saw Indian Americans in need of their tutelage and guidance.

Irony can be found, perhaps, in the fact that since the last decade of the twentieth century, Western nations have launched a movement toward "restorative justice," toward substituting restitution and reconciliation for punishment. For examples to study, they have turned to those societies still practicing traditional law.

Notes

[1] We will use the terms "traditional" and "customary" interchangeably.

[2] A moiety is one of two complementary divisions of a tribe or village.

Chapter Seven

The U.S.
Legal System

"We're just here to try a case, we're not here to practice law!"

(Merry, 1986:259)

Anthropologists studying the U.S. legal system have concentrated on two areas. One is the way the system works in practice, as opposed to descriptions of how it is supposed to work. The second area concerns the ways in which ordinary people—as opposed to social or political elites—make use of the system.

The quote at the head of this chapter is an outburst from a frustrated defense attorney. It was captured by an anthropologist observing how residents of a multiethnic, low-income American neighborhood made use of the lower civil and criminal courts. The attorney's comment pithily summed up the anthropologist's conclusion that the U.S. legal system offered two competing ideologies of law.

After several years of observing court proceedings as well as interviewing both court personnel and neighborhood residents, Sally Merry (1986) found that people generally turned to courts for help in solving interpersonal problems that they had not been able to resolve in other ways. Once they entered the court system, they encountered a formal theory of justice, but also an informal one.

Merry saw that people seeking the court's help did so based on their understanding of the formal theory, one that said that people had legal rights, that all people were equal before the law, that these rights are routinely enforced by police and courts, and that the state takes violations of law seriously. "To be accused of a violation of the law is a serious and frightening event, and to make accusations of others is to invoke a powerful weapon" (1986:257).

Merry's informants found this philosophy of legal rights appealing, even though they did not have accurate knowledge of exactly which rights were protected by law. She found that people sought legal relief when someone insulted them or made faces at them, although U.S. law provides little protection from such actions. They were sure that they had total rights against trespassers, although the law says that property owners are obligated to keep their property free from hazards that might harm, or even entice, trespassers, such as an unfenced swimming pool. They did not understand such legal niceties as "duty to mitigate." When a tenant moved out of his apartment 10 days after the beginning of the month without paying the entire month's rent, the landlord took him to small claims court. The landlord was outraged to learn that the law demanded that he first try to reduce his losses by attempting to rent the apartment as soon as it was vacant.

In addition to encountering the intricacies of the formal theory, clients of the courts also came up against the informal or "situational" theory of justice. In this theory, enforcement is not automatic; the justice system must be triggered by complaints. Merry's informants also found that not all incidents bearing the same legal label—e.g., assault—received the same treatment. Two types of factors influenced the court's response. The first type is personal; everyone is not handled the same way. People who are working and supporting their families, people who have not been in trouble with the law, people who have not filed claims before—these people will be treated with greater seriousness and respect than those who do not meet these criteria. The second factor concerns the context of the complaint, especially the relationship between or among the disputing parties. Disputes between relatives, acquaintances, or neighbors are considered trivial, even if they involve genuine loss or injury. Parties in cases like these are constantly pressured to settle in ways that do not involve the court—by discussion, negotiation, or mediation.

Merry makes it clear that one of these theories is not "truer" than the other. Both are true and courthouse personnel—judges, prosecutors, defense attorneys, clerks, and probation officers—operate in a world that recognizes both cultures and the tension between them (1986:258). Proceedings in juvenile cases provide an example of the ways in which judges can manipulate the two theories. Children who run away from home or do not attend school can be charged as *status offenders* by parents, police, or school officials. Judges hearing such a case may find the child "in need of services" and assign custody of the child to the state's Department of Social Services (DSS). The department may eventually decide to remove the child from the parental home. This actually happens in less than a quarter of the cases; nevertheless, judges often threaten rebellious juveniles with removal and placement, although in reality all a judge can do is assign custody to DSS. On the other hand, frustrated parents who come to the court asking it to take custody of their child are told that juveniles are rarely placed in a foster home or a juvenile facility and that such placement is actually very difficult to arrange. The judge uses the formal theory in attempting to control the juvenile but uses the "situational" theory to discourage to parents from pursuing the charge, a process that could lead to a time-consuming court process and an expensive placement (1986:263–264).

Another type of situation develops when parties to a case are operating on different theories of justice. An elderly couple was upset about the amount of noise neighborhood children were making when they played ball in the street. The couple found that there was actually a local ordinance against playing ball in the street; they started calling the police every time the children came out to play, often several times a day. Tired of these constant drains on their time, police officers informed the children's parents that the ordinance was a very old one and only enforced when a complaint was made. They suggested that the parents sue the couple for harassment. When this came to the attention of the police chief, he insisted that no officer of his would ever make such a suggestion. The complaining couple based their actions on the formal theory of justice—the law gave them certain rights to quiet, and when the law was broken the system responded automatically that offenders would be punished and order restored. The parents based their response on the situational theory—not all laws are important, enforcement takes place only when someone demands that it take place, and making that demand unreasonably is itself cause for legal action. The police officers reinforced the parents' situational theory, but the chief felt compelled to voice only the formal theory.

Like the elderly couple in this example, most plaintiffs began their use of the courts naively, relying only on the theory of formal justice. As a result, they were often disappointed and unhappy with the outcome. However, their disappointment did not necessarily keep them from returning to the courts, especially if they found that other strategies, such as counseling, negotiation, or mediation, were not more satisfactory. As they became more experienced users of the courts, Merry found, some came to understand the existence of the two theories of justice and were able to predict which would apply under differing sets of circumstances. "Defendants and plaintiffs who recognize the duality of ideologies in the court and the nature of the linkage between them can become as sophisticated as court officials in the courthouse game. They become increasingly effective in harnessing and using the power of the law for their own purposes." They lose their awe of the system as they come to see it as "informal, negotiated, and flexible" (261).

Other studies demonstrate that while the formal legal theory speaks of equality before the law, the situational system treats complainants according to who they are rather than according to what they do. A study of "show cause" hearings in Riverside, a small New England town, provides a telling example. In cases where there has been no arrest, complaints brought by citizens and police are heard by the court clerk. It is the clerk, who need not have formal legal training, who determines whether the complaints are serious enough to warrant a formal criminal charge and the issuance of a warrant. Only when a warrant is issued does a complaint formally enter the court system (Yngvesson 1990).

Complaints brought by the Riverside police generally result in the speedy production of a warrant. The clerk perceives the very presence of a police officer as testimony to the seriousness of the case. Police complaints usually concern property offenses between strangers rather than assaults between neighbors or family members; police try to handle the latter cases "on the street" or else send them directly to the clerk. Clerk and police evaluate quarrels between intimates the same way—as "garbage" cases that do not belong in the legal system (Yngvesson 1990:470). According to the clerk, hearings divide situations that can be resolved with everyday commonsense from those that deserve the attention of the law and the court. This does not mean that residents of the town are powerless in their relationships with the clerk. They can, over time, force the clerk to redefine a situation.

Milltown is a small industrial community in the court's jurisdiction. Most Riverside residents think of the area as a slum, a place where "the other half of America lives" (Yngvesson 1990:473). Milltown residents would come to the clerk with complaints of assaults, threats, or trespassing, most of which described as "children's fights" in which adults became involved as they tried to stop the fighting. The clerk dismissed most of them. As the neighborhood began to gentrify, however, the new homeowners started to define the clashes in terms of neighborhood disorganization. At first, the clerk tried to appeal to common values, pointing out that children would fight and that it was up to parents to control them. He would "technically" issue complaints but "hold" them, ready to dismiss them if there were no more trouble. After a while, however, the clerk began to accept the residents' definition of the situation.

> Through the appropriation by upwardly mobile residents of an imagery of chaos in which knife-wielding children were the central figures, the clerk was persuaded over two years of repeated complaints brought by the same individuals that the neighborhood needed attention. (474)

The clerk issued the desired warrants and the complaints entered the criminal justice system.

All of these studies reveal how much of the legal process takes place outside of the courtroom. Attorneys, court clerks, and mediators define law every bit as much as do legislators and judges. A comparative study of language patterns makes the same point in a different way.

Procedures in U.S. courts are formal and orderly. Attorneys may speak only when called upon by the judge or when deferred to by the opposing attorney ("Your witness, counselor"). Witnesses speak only to answer questions put by attorneys. Speakers do not "overlap" or begin speaking before someone else has finished. This carefully ordered speaking arrangement makes it possible for everything that is said during the proceeding to be heard by everybody else and for all speech to be easily recorded.

The ordered speaking style of the U.S. courtroom has been contrasted with the style of the *panchayat*, or community court, of

India. In that forum, there is neither a predetermined order of speakers nor a single person with the authority to compel order, so overlapping or simultaneous speech is common. Speakers interrupt each other and one begins before the previous one has finished. But it turns out that the Indian panchayat and the U.S. courtroom do not always have identical functions (Hayden 1987). By the time the panchayat assembles, members already agree on the facts of the case; what remains to be decided is the seriousness of the offense and the resulting sanction. The U.S. courtroom, on the other hand, is a fact-finding venue. The main purpose of a trial is to find out what actually happened. The "evaluative function"—how serious was the offense and what is the appropriate sanction—takes place in the jury room or in the judge's chambers.

Robert Hayden reminds us that the majority of cases in the United States do not come to trial. They are plea-bargained because, just as with panchayat members, the parties are able to agree upon a certain version of the facts and are then prepared to negotiate the sanction. This version of the facts is not necessarily a version that coincides with some objective version of the truth. It must only satisfy all parties sufficiently that they may continue to the final phase of the proceeding. In both cases, what takes place behind the scenes is at least as important as what takes place in the public forum. Observations of plea-bargaining sessions—the evaluative function—lead to the conclusion that they are just as prone to overlap and interruption as the panchayat.

Chapter Eight

Law as a Tool of Acculturation and Domination

If law is a method of enforcing certain norms and behaviors, it should come as no surprise that law is a method by which one group can enforce its norms and behaviors on others. The colonial situation provides a special case and numerous instances for examining this function of law. Because colonial nations wielded great power over the lands that they conquered, colonial administrators were not reluctant to develop and enforce rules that benefited themselves, often at great cost to the conquered people. But neither conquerors nor conquered were ever monolithic; within each there were various interest groups that reacted differently to the laws of the imperial government. And even with the might of an empire behind them, laws do not enforce themselves. Furthermore, colonial settlers were often greatly outnumbered by their subjects and, in addition, might have had their own reasons for ignoring certain laws promulgated by their own governments.

Colonial powers enacted laws that served different needs. One category of laws had an economic base. Some of this legislation molded indigenous people into a capitalistic labor force by "punishing failure to work, outlawing festivals and other entertainments (such as cockfighting) that distracted from work, prohibiting alcoholic beverages, controlling vagabondage, and defining criminality (Merry 1992:364).

Other economically motivated laws restricted local people's access to natural resources or taxed the subjugated people in terms of goods, money, or labor. But simple exploitation of a conquered people does not necessarily call for law. Law may appear to legitimate the colonial appropriation of resources, it may allocate those resources among groups within the colonialist nation, and it may mediate among conflicting values presented by the colonialist situation. The Spanish *encomienda* (discussed in detail in the next section) provides an example of the way in which law was used in an attempt to reconcile the economic imperatives of imperialism, the Catholic Church's desire to convert the native people of the Americas, the demands of the Spanish explorers to be compensated for the risks they encountered, and the Spanish Crown's fear of an emerging colonial aristocracy.

Another set of motivations for enacting law involved Western morality. Over and over again, colonial rulers found themselves scandalized, shocked, or outraged by local customs, customs that they labeled "pagan," "uncivilized," or "indecent." These included the breast-revealing clothing of Hawaiian women; New Guinea headhunting; concubinage in Hong Kong; and the suttee of India, which demanded that a widow throw herself upon her husband's funeral pyre. Declaring such customs illegal and punishing those who broke the law was not only a way of eliminating the customs, but also of expressing the moral superiority of the lawmakers.

A third set of motivations reflects a desire to acculturate the indigenous people and force them to participate in Western culture; one way of doing this was to destroy the native culture by, among other tactics, outlawing its most important practices, practices colonialists saw as primitive and inferior. Although such lawmakers were thoroughly ethnocentric, they were not necessarily racist, since they believed indigenous people were capable of participating fully in Western culture, a culture they assumed to be the pinnacle of human achievement. In the United States, this attitude was expressed in the phrase, "killing the Indian in order to save the man," and resulted in such institutions as the Indian boarding schools. Federal officials forced Native American children to attend these schools, which were usually far from their homes. Teachers administered corporal punishment to students speaking languages other than English or for any other manifestation of their native culture. It is this class of laws that often reflects a clash of values and mutual misunderstanding.

THE ENCOMIENDA

The *conquistadores* who claimed the Americas for the Spanish Crown in the fifteenth and sixteenth centuries were rarely members of the aristocracy. More often they were relatively poor but ambitious men who saw the New World as a source of wealth that would enhance their status and lifestyle when they or their descendents returned to Spain. Central to this image was the labor of the native people, those who Columbus had dubbed *Indians.* It was these people who were to do the mining, building, and agriculture that would produce riches for the returning Spaniards. Slavery seemed the most efficient means for bringing about this goal.

The kings and queens for whom these lands were claimed were also interested in wealth, but to them the Indians were not only sources of labor, they were also new subjects whose interests had to be protected and who could be converted to Christianity. Crown and conquistador agreed that Indians should labor, but they did not agree upon the conditions. Queen Isabela, for example, was devoted to the model of free wage labor, that the Indians should be compensated for their work. But Spain was anxious for the riches of the New World, and the Spanish settlers insisted the Indians would not work if not forced to do so (Simpson 1966).

The encomienda, a system of tribute and labor that had been devised when Spain conquered the Moors (Arabs of North Africa), provided a solution. In Spanish America, the law of encomienda became an attempt to reconcile the disparate visions of the settlers and the Crown and to some extent it did just that, but it also demonstrated some of the weaknesses of law as a method of social control.

The encomienda defined the indigenous people of New Spain as Spanish subjects who, along with other Spanish subjects, owed obedience and tribute to the Spanish government. This was not a new concept to the Indians, many of whom had paid tribute to their Inca or Aztec overlords. But the only commodities the Indians had were their labor and agricultural produce, neither of which was of much use to their majesties in faraway Madrid. Therefore, the Crown would assign Indian labor to Spanish settlers who would use it to produce goods that would enrich them and would eventually benefit Spain itself. In return, the settlers would see to the welfare of the Indians, pay them decent wages, and allow the clergy to instruct them in Christianity. The labor would be forced, but it would be compensated.

The Spanish were able to justify this arrangement because of their conviction that the native people were fundamentally lazy and would do nothing without proper direction. "The Indian loved to go about naked and they held money and property as no value . . . they had no sense of shame . . . they had no feeling of guilt" (Simpson 1966:46). The *encomenderos* were to clothe and educate the natives, bring them to Christianity, and force them to abandon their pagan culture.

Greed and the declining Indian population undermined these relatively humanitarian inclinations: overwork, underpayment, and enslavement never disappeared. Although a number of governors sent from Spain tried to enforce the laws of the encomienda, they were no match for the settlers. Occasionally Indians found more powerful allies in some of the Spanish clergy who saw themselves as the protectors of these new or potential Christians. At least some clergy demanded that the settlers provide better treatment to the Indians or suffer the pains of eternal damnation. But the clergy did not ignore earthly law entirely. In 1512, Dominican friars persuaded King Ferdinand to pass the Laws of Burgos, a set of standards for pay and working conditions, as well as supervision by royal officials. Again, greed and distance overwhelmed humanitarian inclinations, since there were too few royal officials to enforce them. The Laws of Burgos remained on the books, but they were ignored (Bannon 1966).

If the Spanish government was concerned for the welfare of its Indian subjects, it was also concerned for its own well-being. Spain was only now emerging from a feudalism in which the power of the great lords and landowners easily rivaled the power of the throne. The settlers of New Spain were beginning to form *haciendas*, large self-sufficient landholdings worked by Indians. Because the rights of the encomienda could be passed from father to son, the encomenderos presented the threat of becoming a new hereditary feudal aristocracy, a class that could easily be a threat to the central government of a Spain only recently united by Ferdinand and Isabella.

In 1541, King Charles V presented all the problems of the encomienda to a special council, which decided that the institution was open to great abuse, inherently unjust, and should be abolished. The New Laws of 1542 were an attempt to phase it out gradually and, in doing so, to meet the needs of church, government, and settlers. It stated that no new encomiendas would be established. It secured the position of the Crown by providing that encomiendas could not be inherited; upon the death of an encomendero, the tribute that the Indians had been paying to him would now be paid directly to the government.

The New Laws provoked riots in some parts of the Spanish Empire and simple disdain in others. Again, the government proved too weak, too distant, and too dependent on the wealth that the settlers provided to enforce the hated provisions. Again, the laws were not repealed, but allowed to lapse.

Unable to abolish the encomienda, the government concentrated on weakening it. In 1549 it insisted that tribute be paid in kind, not in labor. Some years later Spanish officials decreed that the tribute should be paid directly to the government, which would then redistribute part of it to the encomenderos, thereby forcing the settlers out of the relationship between Crown and Indians. Still too weak to eradicate the inheritance provisions, the Spanish government limited them to two or three generations, thereby eliminating the threat of a hereditary aristocracy. Finally, it replaced the encomienda with the *repartimiento,* a system whereby local government officials assigned Indians to work on projects deemed to be for the public good.

The repartimiento itself was liable to abuse and the definition of "public good" often had a distinctly private aspect to it. Government officials—paid by and therefore theoretically loyal to the Crown—were few in number and often corrupt or lazy. Many churchmen labored hard to protect the Indians from exploitation. Others believed that they were doing the Indians a favor by introducing them to Catholicism and tutoring them in the ways of "civilization," and that those favors should be repaid in labor and goods. When the Indians saw it differently, force would be applied. The Spanish government's humanitarian impulses were always undermined, first by its distance and impotence, and later by its increasing reliance on the silver and gold excavated from its empire. The laws of the encomienda did help to mediate the conflicting and changing interests of Church, Crown, Indian, and encomendero, but the inability to enforce the law always lagged behind the law's ambitions.

THE LAW AGAINST THE POTLATCH

> Every Indian or other person who engages in or assists in cele-
> brating the Indian festival known as the "Potlatch" or in the
> Indian dance known as the "Tamanawas" is guilty of a misde-
> meanor, and shall be liable to imprisonment for a term of not
> more than six nor less than two months in any gaol or other
> place of confinement; and any Indian or other person who
> encourages, either directly or indirectly, an Indian or Indians to
> get up such a festival or dance, or to celebrate the same, or who
> shall assist in the celebration of same is guilty of a like offense,
> and shall be liable to the same punishment. (Section 3 of the
> *Indian Act* 1884)

The native peoples of the Northwest Coast of North America carried out changes of status in public with events featuring feasting,
dancing, and gift giving (Cole and Chaiken 1990). The host of such an
event used it to proclaim his right to certain ranks, titles, and privi-
leges. An important part of the *potlatch* ceremony was elaborate ora-
tory, in which the claimant detailed the origin and history of the
status in question, as well as the heredity and virtue that justified his
claim. The guests who participated in the activities and accepted the
gifts bestowed upon them validated these claims. In turn, their own
status was publicly legitimated by the value of the gifts they received,
by the order in which the gifts were presented, and often by their
place in the seating arrangements. Prestige was a function of generosity, which meant that anyone receiving extensive gifts at a potlatch
needed to repay with an even grander potlatch at a future date.

The potlatch was a complex institution and had variations
among tribes, but there were certain common features. Potlatches
were held to settle questions of rank, status, and precedence; they
composed an intricate network of gifts and repayments; and they
had a strong spiritual dimension. Potlatch givers needed depen-
dents and retainers to supply the wealth needed to host the event;
potlatches provided for the exchange and redistribution of
resources; they required months and even years of preparation.
Because major potlatches involved people from many different villages, they offered opportunities for trade, socializing, and the
arrangement of marriages. They were a major source of entertain-
ment during the winter months.

Among the tribes that practiced the potlatch were the Coast Salish of Washington state and the Tlingit, Chilkat, and Gitskan of Alaska. Most potlatching, however, took place in Canada, in the area that was to become the province of British Columbia, which was home not only to sections of these tribes, but also to the Haida, Tsimshian, Kwakiutl, and Nootka. The economy of these areas depended on hunting, fishing, and gathering. The abundance of natural resources meant that the Northwest Coast people did not have to travel in search of food, but could settle in permanent villages where they built large wooden houses and developed a rich and varied artistic tradition. They were able to accumulate and store a surplus of food and other goods and it was this wealth that made the potlatch possible. Unlike many hunting and gathering societies, those of the Northwest Coast were not egalitarian, but instead consisted of a number of social classes, with the upper classes being divided into gradations of rank. One's place in such a society was dictated partly by heredity and partly by one's ability to claim the rank that heredity made possible.

Initial contact between Northwest Coast natives and European trappers and traders intensified the potlatch. From the time of Captain Cook's first visit to the area (1778), Europeans were anxious to obtain the furs that the Indians were able to supply. The fur trade provided a new source of wealth for the local communities and much of this wealth went into potlatches, which appear to have increased in both number and size.

Trappers and traders came and went. Settlers stayed. The discovery of gold in 1858 brought an influx of miners, many of whom would stay to become farmers, commercial fishers, and entrepreneurs—people determined to re-create the societies they had known in Europe and in eastern Canada. Missionaries, equally determined to convert the native people to Christianity, accompanied them. The potlatch became a lightening rod for clashing assumptions and values. What makes it particularly interesting, however, is the fact that neither Native nor Euro-Canadian groups were ever in total agreement about the value of the potlatch and, within each group, attitudes changed over time.

Many early white observers of the potlatch responded positively. They enjoyed the dances and the opportunity to see the Indians in their festive garb. Collectors of native art and artifacts seized the opportunity for new acquisitions. Traders and merchants quickly recognized that the increasing wealth that went into potlatching provided economic opportunities for them. Missionaries, however, saw the potlatch with its connection to native spiritual beliefs as an obstacle to their work of conversion. Government agents understood that as the custom reinforced the status of native chiefs and nobility, it undermined the government's attempts to impose its own authority. As ranching, mining, and commercial fishing came to rely on Indian labor, owners of these enterprises resented the time and energy that went into the potlatch.

Nor were the people of the First Nations always united in their support of potlatching. While the majority regarded the potlatch as an integral and beneficial part of their culture, those at the bottom of the status system often saw it as oppressive, since the fruits of their labor went to benefit their chiefs, not themselves. Converts to Christianity rejected it for religious reasons, while some native people drawn into the cash economy did not have the time for the extensive travel and many days consumed by the event. Many tribes were willing to drop those aspects whites found most offensive—ritual or actual cannibalism being the most common example—but wished to retain the rest.

At bottom, disagreement over the potlatch represented differing values. All involved acknowledged that there was a relationship between wealth and status, but they disagreed as to the nature of that relationship. To Euro-Canadians, status resulted from the accumulation and investment of wealth. Wealth bought fishing boats and trade goods, land and labor. These, in turn, produced more wealth. To native Canadians, on the other hand, status resulted from the dispersal of wealth and the return of what is today referred to as "social capital." The greater one's reputation for generosity, the greater the number of people in one's debt, the higher the status. What was to the Indians an investment in their social position was, to the Euro-Canadians, a wicked waste of potential productivity.

The law against the potlatch had a number of aims. Outlawing a custom that was an important part of the native religion should make it easier to convert native people to Christianity. Eliminating long, large gatherings under unsanitary conditions was meant to improve health and facilitate the school attendance of children. Doing away with the elaborate system of payments and repayments would free the Indians to work in Euro-Canadian owned fisheries and farms. Undermining the hierarchy of status and rank would undermine native social structure, making it easier to assimilate the Indians into the white culture. All this could be accomplished by taking an integral part of native culture and turning it into a crime.

From the time of its passage in 1880, native people tried to get the law against potlatches revoked. When that proved ineffective, they resorted to subterfuges. They would hold potlatches in remote places, posting guards to warn if police officers approached. They would have singing and dancing on one occasion and gift giving on another, thereby technically not really having a potlatch. Or they would hold potlatches on birthdays, Christmas, or other holidays, proclaiming that they were simply celebrating in the way of the white man.

The weight of the law, combined with changing economic realities, changed the potlatch. It became shorter and less extravagant. The status hierarchy was no longer as clear cut. Cannibalism disappeared. Finally, the law was quietly dropped from the penal code in 1951.

SUTTEE

The custom of allowing, encouraging, or forcing widows to be buried with their husbands was quite widespread. It seems to have been practiced by the Vikings, as well as by Egyptian and Chinese nobility. Today it is best known from its practice in India, a practice outlawed by the British in 1829.

Suttee (or *sati*) was the rite in which a widow was burned alive on her husband's funeral pyre. The assumption was that she did this voluntarily, out of love for him and by her willingness to ensure, by her death, salvation for them both. Indeed, it was the formal duty of everyone close to a new widow to attempt to talk her out of ritual suicide. Nevertheless, the social pressures were so strong that some women did go to their deaths willingly. Others did not and might be forced to the pyre and even tied to it so that they would not escape.

Hindu scholars report that there is nothing in the Hindu sacred writings that encourages suttee (Mani 1987:137). Nevertheless, it had become an accepted part of Hindu culture, and a widow who performed it brought great honor to herself, her husband, and her family. It is still possible to see shrines erected to such pious and faithful widows.

Indian society had no place for a woman who outlived her husband. Forbidden to remarry, she remained the dependent of her husband's family, which regarded her as simply another mouth to feed. The fear that she would disgrace the family by sexual impropriety did not always prevent male members of the household from sexually abusing a young widow. Her existence was a social and economic inconvenience to others and often a burden to herself. Suttee solved all these problems. It is important to point out, however, that the vast majority of Hindu widows did not perform suttee and that the custom was concentrated in only a few states.

The British initially operated in India through the British East India Company, an organization of merchants who came to India in 1600 to take part in the spice trade. The company negotiated with the rulers of the various Indian states, first for the right to trade, then to build factories and forts. Through a combination of wealth, guile, and force, the British came to rule all of Asia between present-day Afghanistan and Myanmar. In North America, where they had come to establish permanent settlements, the British either had to eliminate the original occupants of the land or else "civilize" them into compatible neighbors. In India, by contrast, as long as the population provided labor and did not rebel, the company felt no need to interfere in the local culture. Several customs did put this early version of cultural relativism to the test—these included polygamy, child marriage, and suttee.

The British were not the first to be morally offended by suttee. The Mughal emperor Akbar (1542–1605) tried hard to discourage it. The Hindu reformer Ram Mohan Roy (1772–1833) campaigned energetically against it, and it may have been Roy who brought it to the attention of the William Bentinck, who became governor-general of the East India Company in 1828 (Mani 1987:138).

Bentinck provided an interesting account of the reasoning that led him to declare suttee a crime. His first fear was that to abandon the policy of tolerance of local custom in one instance would lead the Indian population to suspect that the British were planning to abolish it in other areas also. While this suspicion might not lead to armed rebellion, it would lead to distrust of all other efforts, such as European education, intended for the improvement of the Indian people. Bentinck was also aware that stability was necessary for the trade that had brought the British to India in the first place.

Bentinck discounted the possibility of armed rebellion by noting that the majority of suttees in the previous years occurred in the provinces of Bengal, Behar, and Orissa and the majority of these took place in the area around Calcutta. He explained that the people of this area have such a "want of courage and of vigour of character" and that such is "the habitual submission of centuries" that he did not fear insurrection. He pragmatically admitted that if suttee had been more widespread in those provinces where the population was more "bold and manly" he might have proceeded with less confidence. He then declared that this law would improve the morality of the Hindus as well as their "conception of the will of God" by dissociating religion from "blood and murder." He ended with a proclamation that outlawing suttee was consistent with the mission and noble example of the British Empire, an empire that would be permanently stained if it tolerated this immoral practice (Bentinck 1929).

When an independent India revised its penal code in the 1950s, it did not mention suttee explicitly. "The presumption was that its sections on murder and abetment to suicide . . . would be enough to deal with such a happening. . . . This implicit redefinition of sati as a crime is accepted by women opposed to the custom—they deem it to be murder or abetted suicide" (Oldenberg 1994:102).

Suttee provides additional proof that outlawing a custom does not abolish the custom. Reports of the practice diminished but continued through the twentieth century (Oldenburg 1994), and the diminution was probably due as much to the teachings of Roy and Gandhi as to the law. Nor did abolishing suttee abolish the conditions that supported it (Seabrook 2002). In parts of India widows are still stigmatized, considered bad luck, and subject to caste rules that forbid them to remarry. Today, as for the past 500 years, the city of Vrindavan is known as the City of Widows, for the thousands of women who make it their home. All have renamed themselves "Dasi," meaning servant. With no job skills or family support, they try to earn a scant living by chanting at one of the city's 4,000 temples to the god Krishna. Many live in the streets and under stairwells, and it is not unusual for their children to turn to begging or crime (Reuters 2003).

These examples show the strengths and weaknesses of law as a tool of acculturation and domination. The law harnessed American

Indian labor for the benefit of the encomenderos and the Spanish Crown. The potlatch survives, but in a far smaller version and with many of its former functions gone. Suttee has largely, although not entirely, vanished from India. On the other hand, encomenderos regularly ignored a law that the government was too weak to enforce. The potlatch was practiced in one form or another throughout the period of its banning and is today considered an integral part of Native Canadian identity. Suttees' almost complete disappearance from India may be due more to the teaching of Indian reformers and philosophers than to British law. Perhaps what these examples show is that law can indeed be an effective tool in some situations, but resistance can at least blunt its edge.

Chapter Nine

Cultural Pluralism and the Cultural Defense

Both lawyers and social scientists are interested in cases in which law and culture clash in the courtroom or the legislature. This can happen even in relatively homogeneous societies, when courts are forced to choose one value over another. For example, Americans tend to value the preservation of life, but they also value privacy and the right of individuals to control their own lives.

In 2005 these values came into conflict over the case of Theresa Schiavo, a 41-year-old woman who had suffered massive brain damage 15 years earlier and ever since had been in what doctors refer to as a "persistent vegetative state." Feeding tubes provided nutrition and hydration to her body. Her husband, contending that she had made it clear that she would not want to live under these conditions, asked for the feeding tubes to be removed. Ms. Schiavo's parents insisted that with the proper treatment she could still recover. Although the vast majority of doctors, including one appointed by the court, disagreed, the parents appealed for the tubes to be left in place. The ensuing protracted legal battle saw both the president of the United States and a majority of the members of Congress insisting that life should be prolonged under any conditions whatsoever. The case finally ended with court decisions in favor of Mr. Schiavo, and the tubes were removed. Although the court decisions ended this particular case, they did nothing to resolve the bitterness on both sides.

These same values of privacy and individual rights had come into conflict 25 years before. In 1973, the Supreme Court of the United States was asked to decide *Roe v. Wade* (410 U.S. 113, 1973) concerning the right of a woman to have an abortion. In its decision, the Court favored a woman's right to privacy and control of her body, but qualified it by saying that in the later stages of pregnancy, the state's interest in protecting prenatal life must be considered. Those whose hierarchy of values placed privacy and individual control ahead of the protection of the fetus were generally pleased with the decision, but those who valued unborn human life ahead of a woman's right to control her body were outraged.

In both cases, religious beliefs about when human life begins and ends played and continue to play a major role in the debates. Similar beliefs about "life" affect the controversy concerning the use of embryonic stem cells for medical research that might provide cures for numerous diseases. Embryonic stem cells are derived from embryos that are developed from eggs that have been fertilized outside of a woman's body. This is commonly done in infertility clinics, where some of the fertilized eggs are implanted in the body of a woman who has been unable to become pregnant in any other way. The procedure involves fertilizing more eggs than are actually used, and the extra eggs are usually destroyed. Instead, people who value the eggs' role in prolonging lives want them to be used for medical research. However, those who believe that these embryos are human and need protection would like to have those beliefs enacted into laws that forbid such research. Opposing such laws are those who believe that these miniscule balls of cells are not human and that depriving the world of the benefits that research might bring is in no way "pro-life."

CULTURAL PLURALISM

Perhaps even more intriguing are cases in which the values of a religious or cultural minority are incompatible with laws that reflect the values of the majority. Nations such as Canada and the United States—nations that are today composed largely of immigrants from different parts of the world—need to create a national culture that will unify these disparate groups. At the same time, they need to protect the human rights of these groups by allowing them a certain amount of autonomy in following their customs and religions. In addition, such nations may also prize the cultural richness that comes from diversity. Some people in the United States use the metaphor of the *melting pot*, suggesting the nation's culture is the result of contributions from all groups. It is clear, however, that not everything added to the cultural melting pot is actually assimilated. Canada has favored the metaphor of the *mosaic*, with a whole that is made up of many different, observable, and respected parts. The inevitable tension that results from trying to balance the need for unity with the desire for diversity has often been a matter for the courts.

Nations that previously saw relatively little immigration are now also facing these tensions. European nations that had once invited "guest workers" from developing nations found that many of these supposedly temporary immigrants did not return home; they remained in the host country, sent for their wives, and soon had European-born children. The end of colonialism saw people from the Caribbean, Africa, and the Middle East looking for greater opportunities in the nations that had once been their colonial masters. The collapse of the Soviet Union forced people out of some of the states of Central Europe, such as Bosnia, Chechnya, and Croatia, in order to escape war and economic devastation. In many cases, the host country found itself unprepared for a sizable minority with its own distinct culture. In order to handle these tensions, governments have often turned to law.

Norwegians assumed that their immigrant Muslim population would, over time, intermarry with Norwegian natives and assimilate into Norwegian culture. Instead, large numbers of young Norwegian-born Muslims—mainly women—were partners in arranged marriages with spouses from their family's home countries such as Morocco and Pakistan (Bawer 2003). Norway's policy of family reunification allows foreign-born spouses of Norwegian residents to bypass many immigration hurdles. Indeed, the Norwegian partners in such arranged marriages are sometimes referred to as "living visas." If the marriages are unhappy, Norwegian law gives husband and wife equal rights of divorce, but many Muslims consider only Muslim divorces legitimate and Islamic law makes divorce more difficult for the wife than for the husband. There is an exception: the marriage contract that accompanies every Muslim marriage may include a clause giving equal right of divorce to the wife.

Norwegians fear that the constant influx of spouses from Muslim countries is a barrier to assimilation (Bawer 2003). They also fear for the success of the marriage. European-born Muslim women tend to have some experience of personal freedom while their foreign-born husbands may expect a wife to be subservient. While some arranged marriages are no doubt happy, Bruce Bawer cites a report from the Oslo-based Human Rights Service stating that others range from loveless to abusive.

Norway passed what seems to be a simple law to deal with this situation. It says that no family reunification through marriage would be permitted unless the marriage contract grants the wife the right of divorce. But not all Norwegians are happy with the law. Some believe it does not go far enough in dealing with the rights of women and the isolation of the Islamic community. Others say it is an unwarranted intrusion into the culture of Norway's Muslim residents, an intrusion not visited upon other ethnic or religious groups. Both points of view reflect the fact that law is not always an effective tool in dealing with the tensions of cultural pluralism (Bawer 2003).

This tension reflected in the Norwegian situation appears in the courtroom in a number of different situations. It can appear when religious or cultural minorities ask to be exempt from certain laws, claiming that the laws are contrary to their history or their religious teachings. It can appear when parties who have made an agreement according to the rules of their culture ask courts to settle a resulting dispute. And it can appear when immigrants accused of a crime point out that their actions were accepted or even compulsory in the lands from which they came. The first two situations force the courts to confront *cultural pluralism,* a nation with several cultures but only one legal system. The third situation introduces the *cultural defense,* a legal strategy that requests leniency for lawbreakers who act according to the dictates of the culture in which they were raised.

Cultural pluralism does not always involve recent immigrants. Groups with a long history in a country may have special standing when it comes to exemption from certain laws. A well-known case involves the Amish request to be exempt from Wisconsin's law on compulsory education. There are approximately 135,000 Old Order Amish in the United States. The Amish started as a reform group within the Mennonite movement in the seventeenth century. In the early eighteenth century some began to immigrate from

Switzerland and the southern Rhine area of Europe to North America, taking up William Penn's offer of religious freedom in the colony of Pennsylvania. Today there are Amish communities in 22 states as well as in southwestern Ontario.

The Amish are conservative Christians who believe God will reward with salvation those who live a life that each day brings an individual closer to the image of Christ. This means living apart from the rest of the world and obeying the rules of the community. Among themselves they speak a German dialect and dress distinctively, with broad brimmed hats for the men and bonnets and aprons for the women. Integral to their beliefs is an agricultural life, since they hold that closeness to the soil brings them closer to God. They do not use power machinery, driving a horse and buggy and tilling the soil with draft horses and rejecting both automobiles and most farm machinery. They reject materialism and consumerism and their austere lifestyle has allowed them to prosper enough to extend their family farms at a time when other small farmers have had to sell out to agribusiness (Kidder and Hostetler 1990:903). Because they do not call upon public assistance, refuse to air their disputes outside of the community, and rarely get arrested for crimes, they are often perceived as model citizens, continuing a rural way of life that the rest of the United States has both abandoned and romanticized.

Amish culture has also brought the Amish community into conflict with the law. The Amish do not consider themselves pacifists, since this would involve them in political action to promote peace (www.religioustolerance.org/amish2.htm). However, since they do refuse to resort to violence or take up arms, they must reject any involvement with the military. During World War I, both Canada and the United States instituted a draft. Canada gave the Amish and other conscientious objectors leaves of absence. Although the U.S. legislation recognized the status of conscientious objector, there was no method for implementing it. Amish boys were called to military duty and most refused to go. Some were physically and mentally abused in an effort to get them to join the armed forces.

By the time of the Second World War, the Amish, Mennonites, Quakers, and other religious groups had prevailed upon their governments to institutionalize the status of conscientious objectors (COs). The Canadian Alternative Service Work Plan (ASW) and the American Civil Public Service (CPS) program permitted COs to be given work assignments outside of the military. In the post-World War II years, Amish men could choose between the draft and two years of alternative service. By the 1960s, Amish communities in the United States were finding that about half of the young men performing alternative service never returned to their communities. So they organized the National Amish Steering Committee to attempt to negotiate another arrangement with the federal government, and in 1969, they agreed upon a system of "farm deferments," allowing Amish draftees to substitute agricultural work for their military obligations.

The Amish belief in reliance upon the community rather than the government has caused other conflicts. They have refused to take part in programs of unemployment insurance, Medicare, social security, or the Canadian Pension Plan. When in 1955 the government of the United States expanded Social Security to cover self-employed farmers, the Amish refused to pay into the system, since their beliefs called upon them to care for the old people of their families and communities themselves. On several occasions the government placed liens on Amish farms and sometimes went so far as to foreclose and sell the property for back social security taxes. Government agents accosted one Amish farmer while he was plowing his fields; they confiscated his three horses (Hostetler 1993:276). It was the indignation of his non-Amish neighbors that stopped such actions and again brought about negotiation. Amish religious leaders went to Washington to ask that they be exempted from both the payments and the benefits of the Social Security program. In 1965, Congress passed legislation that granted the Amish this exemption.

The history of groups like the Amish and the Society of Friends (Quakers) go back to the earliest days of colonial America, and both groups are viewed as being productive and respectable. Legislatures have thus tended to defer to their requests, such as that for CO status. But even the Amish have not been able to keep all their conflicts with the law out of the courts. The most famous case involving the Amish concerns compulsory education.

Amish culture actually depends upon a certain level of education. Not only are literacy and a certain level of mathematical skills required for commercial farming, but the ability to read the Bible is necessary for Amish spiritual life. These skills were traditionally taught in rural, one-room schoolhouses where the student body was entirely Amish and where the community had control over the curriculum. In addition to basic skills, children learned to value manual labor, cooperation, and the importance of separation from the world and worldly things.

In the latter half of the twentieth century, a number of developments threatened this arrangement. One was a movement toward school consolidation, resulting in few and larger schools with greater diversity in the student body. A second was increasing state control over the choice of teachers, textbooks, and curricula. Finally, states concerned with producing workers for an increasingly technological society passed laws mandating school attendance until the age of 16. Again, negotiations took place, but in 1973, Wisconsin's compulsory education law landed the Amish in court. Three Amish fathers were convicted and fined when they refused to send their children to school after the eighth grade, claiming that the law interfered with their constitutional right to the free exercise of their religion as well as their right to direct the religious upbringing of their children.

The Supreme Court of the United States ruled in favor of the parents (*Wisconsin v. Yoder* 406 U.S. 205, 1972). Much of the decision was spent praising the Amish way of life. "The Amish community has been a highly successful social unit within our society, even if apart from the conventional 'mainstream.' Its members are productive and very law-abiding members of society; they reject public welfare in any of its usual modern forms."

In response to Wisconsin's argument that curtailing their education would diminish the careers of those children who might later decide to leave the religious community, the Court held:

> There is nothing in this record to suggest that the Amish qualities of reliability, self-reliance, and dedication to work would fail to find ready markets in today's society . . . we are unwilling to assume that persons possessing such valuable vocational skills and habits are doomed to become burdens on society.

Even the state's contention that additional education was necessary if the Amish were to participate effectively in the democratic process was rebuffed.

> Indeed, the Amish communities singularly parallel and reflect many of the virtues of Jefferson's ideal of the 'sturdy yeoman' who would form the basis of what he considered the ideal of a democratic society. Even their idiosyncratic separateness exemplifies the diversity we profess to admire and encourage.

Nevertheless, the Court made it clear that neither diversity nor deeply held values alone would be enough to allow an individual or a group to opt out of the compulsory education law. Its decision placed great emphasis on the Amish community's three centuries as an identifiable religious sect, its long history as a "successful and self-sufficient segment of American society" and "the interrelationship of belief with their mode of life." With this emphasis, the Court moved away from its previous tentative acceptance of religion as an individual's "ultimate concern" and returned to its earlier stress on culture, organization, and history (Donovan and Anderson 2003:101).

Of particular interest to students of law and culture is the unusual deference paid to the expert testimony of anthropologist John Hostetler, who was himself raised in an Amish family (Erickson and Simon 1998:21). Not only does the Court's decision cite his work in several footnotes, it includes in the text his testimony that "'compulsory high school attendance could not only result in great psychological harm to Amish children, but would also,' in his opinion, 'ultimately result in the destruction of the Old Order Amish church community as it exists in the United States today.'" It may be that Hostetler's testimony was indispensable to the Court's conclusion that enforcing the compulsory attendance law would have had negative effects on the entire Amish community (Rosen 1977:564).

The defendants in *Yoder* based their case in large part on the First Amendment to the Constitution of the United States, which forbids the government to "prohibit the free exercise of religion." Cultural minorities asking for special legal treatment have often—but not always—found that the U.S. government has been most respectful of cultural arguments when they include an appeal to religious freedom. Members of the Native American Church, for example, won the right to use peyote as part of their religious rituals, although their victory was the result of a long and contentious battle in both courts and legislatures (Public Law 103-344 of 1994, technically an amendment to the *American Indian Religious Freedom Act of 1978*).

However, pleading the First Amendment did not help the Church of Jesus Christ of Latter-day Saints (Mormons) when it tried to defend its religion's requirement of polygamy. In the 1879 decision in *Reynolds v. United States* (98 U.S. 146), the Supreme Court stated that the government had a right to criminalize a practice that it found "odious," even if a religious group believed that practice to be commanded by God. It is in this case that we find the first declaration of the principle that while the government may not interfere with religious beliefs and opinions, it may forbid religious practices.

THE CULTURAL DEFENSE

The cases above involve instances in which cultural *groups* sought exemptions from laws that were designed to apply to all persons in a state or nation. The criminal law occasionally produces a case in which an *individual* criminal defendant asks for special treatment due to his or her cultural origins: this is referred to as the cultural defense.

"A cultural defense will negate or mitigate criminal responsibility where acts are committed under a reasonable, good-faith belief in their propriety, based upon the actor's cultural heritage or tradition" (Lyman 1986:88). One case that seemed to call for a cultural defense was *State v. Kargar* (679 A.2d 81 Me. 1996). Mr. Kargar, who had immigrated to the United States from Afghanistan, was prosecuted for "gross sexual assault" for kissing the penis of his nine-month-old son. Witnesses testified that Islamic law did not consider such an act to be either wrong or sexual; in fact, by kissing a part of the body that is not considered clean or holy in Islam, Kargar was showing how much he really loved his son. The judge held that regardless of its technical language, the statute was not intended to criminalize nonsexual conduct and "that Kargar's conduct could be deemed nonsexual by virtue of his cultural background." He was found to be not guilty of a crime (Donovan and Anderson 2003:108).

Most observers would join the judge in sympathizing with Kargar in this case and it is one of the few in which the cultural defense was totally effective. Other cases have garnered less sympathy, often because the actions in question resulted in harm to a victim. An example of a far more controversial case is *People v. Chen* (No. 87-7774 N.Y. Sup. Ct. Mar. 21, 1989). Dong Lu Chen had emigrated from China one year earlier, together with his wife of 23 years and their only son. One day Mrs. Chen made some remarks that led Mr. Chen to believe that she was having an extramarital affair. He left the room and returned carrying a hammer, which he used to kill her. He was charged with second-degree murder.

Chen's defense lawyer, with the aid of an anthropologist expert witness, argued that in China a wife's unfaithfulness is an insult to her husband's ancestors and that a husband in this situation is expected to threaten to kill her. They also argued that in China Mr. Chen would have been surrounded by relatives and neighbors who would have intervened and prevented the murder. There was no such community in New York to protect Mrs. Chen.

> In other words, Chen's reaction to the revelations of his wife's infidelities was culturally appropriate. The same cultural script that allowed him to threaten his wife provided interventions that would protect her from real harms. It was the lack of the second component that rendered Chen's reaction tragically dysfunctional. (Donovan and Anderson 2003:109)

The judge found this argument persuasive, sentencing Chen to the lightest possible penalty for second-degree manslaughter.

Many people greeted the sentence with outrage. Women's groups and Asian-American groups filed a complaint with the state Commission on Judicial Conduct. Their message was that the sentence in this case showed that American law would not protect Asian women from violence, even if that violence proved to be lethal. "The overwhelmingly negative reactions to Judge Pincus's decisions in the Chen case raised the question of whether, under the guise of cultural sensitivity, judges are only masking a willingness to undervalue the life of a woman who has committed, or who was believed to have committed, adultery" (Norgren and Nanda 1996:274). Experts on Chinese culture also felt that it had been misrepresented in the testimony presented in court. Contemporary Chinese law strongly condemns domestic violence, and the Chinese government has taken a strong stand against wife abuse. The prosecution was criticized for not presenting its own witnesses who would have given a different interpretation of the Chinese attitude toward spouse abuse. This case clearly raises the question: if a cultural defense is to be raised, what is the proper way for the relevant cultural characteristics to be presented in court?

Kong Moua and Seng Xiong, both members of a Hmong tribe, were born in Laos and came to the United States as teenagers. Kong wished to marry Seng and believed he was following Hmong marriage customs when he abducted her and forced her to have sex with him. A Hmong bride is supposed to demonstrate her virtue by refusing sexual intercourse until she is forced and Seng did just that. Kong

was surprised, therefore, when Seng accused him of rape. Seng testified that she had rejected the traditions of Hmong marriage and that
her protests were genuine. "After hearing the testimonies of the parties and witnesses and reviewing a doctoral dissertation on Hmong
marriage rituals, the judge sentenced the defendant to ninety days in
the county jail. The defendant was also fined $1,000, with $900 presented to the woman as reparation" (Goldstein 1994:150).

Again we see a case in which the victimization of a woman is
justified to an American court by presenting the act as an accepted
part of the defendant's culture. This is not unusual. A disproportionate number of cases in which the courts accept a cultural
defense involve mistreatment of women. Saks (1996) cites a case in
which two Korean youth were acquitted of raping a Korean woman.
The court admitted cultural evidence to show that the fact that she
had accompanied them to a bar was evidence, in Korean culture,
that she had consented to sex. Even when the case involves one man
murdering another, the status of women may be a factor. A Greek
man was acquitted of murdering his daughter's rapist when the
defense used cultural evidence to demonstrate that the rape of a
daughter was such a matter of honor in Greece that a father had to
avenge it. On the other hand, the court excluded cultural evidence
about honor in the case of a Mexican man who murdered as a
response to an insult. The defendant argued that the court should
have applied a "reasonable Mexican male standard" in deciding
whether he had been so provoked that he was obliged to respond
with violence: the Appeals Court disagreed.

In a number of these cases there are doubts about how accu-
rately the cultural context was presented to the court. "Is Hmong
'marriage by capture' a vital cultural institution in Moua's homeland, or is it merely a cultural ideal that is never actually performed?" (Donovan and Anderson 2003:101). Are all Greek men
obliged to avenge their daughters' honor by murder or is that only
one course open to them? Is the behavior under consideration preferred, but not mandatory? Because culture can change over time,
the court has to be sure that the evidence being presented is contemporary. Even in small countries, cultural practices may vary
from place to place, from urban to rural areas, and among ethnic
groups. Cultural evidence based on fieldwork close to the defendant's home and at a time when the defendant was living there is
the most valuable, but it may be the hardest to obtain.

Is there room for a cultural defense in a multicultural nation? Should all immigrants be prepared to live by the laws of their new homeland from the moment they arrive? Should the law condemn people who act in ways that are acceptable or even mandatory in the cultures in which they were raised? Does it matter if the illegal action causes no harm (or what constitutes "harm")? Does accepting a cultural defense mean that there are different standards of justice for different subcultures? Does accepting a cultural defense make a statement about the value of tolerance and cultural pluralism or does it implicitly demean other cultures by suggesting that their members are incapable of acting in ways that are free of violence and abuse?

Both lawyers and social scientists have argued these questions vigorously (e.g., Renteln 2004). A study of the cases in which a cultural defense has been raised shows that it is rarely offered—and even more rarely accepted—as a justification. *Kargar* is one of the few exceptions to this observation. The court decided Mr. Kargar was not guilty of any crime. More often it is offered in mitigation; the defendant admits that he or she committed a crime but asks for leniency because he or she acted according to the rules of his original culture. At this stage in the proceedings—at sentencing—the judge is in a position to take into consideration information about the original culture, the age and date at which the defendant immigrated, and the amount of harm caused by the defendant's actions. If either form of the cultural defense is accepted, both judge and jury are limited by the way in which cultural evidence is presented in court.

Social scientists may act as expert witnesses for the defendant or, less often, for the prosecution. In this case, they are part of a legal team and must present evidence in the light that is most favorable to their client, avoiding to the extent that they honestly can contradictory information and uncertainties. The scientist occasionally may also function as a "friend of the court," offering to educate the court about the culture in question, without offering any opinions on the present case. Here the scientist may be more forthcoming about the ambiguities and uncertainties inherent in the study of culture, but evidence presented in this way may not be useful in helping the court arrive at verdict or sentence. Wearing either hat, the social scientist must face the problem that the adversary system is not the ideal way of arriving at social scientific truth.

Epilogue

The prophecies of what the courts will do in fact, and nothing more pretentious, are what I mean by law.

—Oliver Wendell Holmes

Two themes emerge from the materials covered in this book. One is that the relationship between law and culture is so close that it may be more accurate to speak of law as an integral part of culture, reflecting the same assumptions, values, and interests reflected in every other part. The creation of a juvenile justice system that is separate and very different from that of adults reflects assumptions about the transition from childhood to adulthood. The place of traditional law in any society reflects the differing interests of rural agriculturalists and pastoralists on the one hand and those of educated urbanites on the other. Religious law may control every aspect of the believer's life or it may be ignored when it conflicts with other values, such as individualism, worldly success, or the desire for experience outside of one's religious community.

The second theme is that laws are never stable and self-evident. They are constantly being contested, interpreted, and manipulated. Lawmakers and judges; plaintiffs and defendants; court personnel and community members; interest groups based on kinship, religion, economics, occupation, ethnicity, social class, or gender—all work to bring about a version of the law that works to their benefit. Although Western law has its basis in shared assumptions, not

109

everyone guided by Western law agrees on how it is applied, especially regarding issues like the legal status of abortion, the right to die, and stem cell research. It is no wonder that Oliver Wendell Holmes resigned himself to a definition of law that depends solely on outcome. The problem is, however, that predicting what courts will do is not easy. If it were, far fewer cases would go to trial.

Bibliography

Akers, Ronald L. 1997. *Criminological Theories*. Los Angeles: Roxbury Company.

Ahmed, Akbar. 1988. *Discovering Islam: Making Sense of Muslim History and Society*. New York: Routledge.

Ahmad, Imad-ad-Dean. 2004. *Religion and Female Genital Mutilation*. Retrieved September 6, 2004. http://www.minaret.org.fgm.htm

Anderson, J. N. D. 1957. "Law as a Social Force in Islamic Culture and History." *Bulletin of SOAS* 20:13–40.

Bannon, J. F., ed.1966. *Indian Labor in the Spanish Indies*. Boston: D. C. Heath and Co.

Barton, John, James Gibbs, Victor Li and John Merryman. 1983. *Law in Radically Different Cultures*. St. Paul, MN: West Publishing Company.

Bawer, Bruce. 2003. "A Problem with Muslim Enclaves." *The Christian Science Monitor*. Retrieved November 16, 2004 www.csmonitor.com/2003/0630/p09so1–coop html

Bazemore, Gordon. 2005. "Whom and How Do We Integrate? Finding Community in Restorative Justice." *Criminology and Public Policy* 4:131–148.

Benda-Beckman, Franz von. 1997. "Citizens, Strangers, and Indigenous People." *Law and Anthropology* 9:1–42.

Benda-Beckman, Keebet von and F. Strijbosch, ed. 1986. *Anthropology of Law in the Netherlands: Essays in Legal Pluralism*. Dordrecht: Foris.

Bentinck, William. 1829. "Lord William Bentinck on the Suppression of Sati, 8 November 1829." In *Speeches and Documents on Indian Policy, 1750–1921,* edited by Arthur Keith, pp. 208–226. Retrieved September 16, 2004 *Internet Modern History Sourcebook*. www.Fordham.edu/halsell/mod/1829bentinck.htm.

Bohannan, Paul. 1989. *Justice and Judgement Among the Tiv*. Prospect Heights, IL: Waveland Press.

Bowen, Catherine Drinker. 1957. *The Lion and the Throne*. Boston: Little, Brown.

Bower, Lisa C. 1994. "Queer Acts and the Politics of 'Direct Address': Rethinking Law, Culture, and Community." *Law and Society Review* 28:1009–1034.

Brenneis, Donald Lawrence and Fred. R. Myers, ed. 1984. *Dangerous Words: Language and Politics in the Pacific.* New York: New York University Press.

Cardozo, Benjamin. 1924. *The Growth of the Law.* New Haven, CT: Yale University Press.

Cole, Douglas and Ira Chaiken. 1990. *An Iron Hand Upon the People: The Law Against the Potlatch on the Northwest Coast.* Seattle: University of Washington Press.

Cole, John W. 1977. "Anthropology Comes Part-Way Home: Community Studies in Europe. *Annual Review of Anthropology* 6:349–78.

Comaroff, John and Simon Roberts. 1981. *Rules and Processes: The Cultural Logic of Dispute in an African Context.* Chicago: University of Chicago Press.

Conley, John and William O'Barr. 1998. *Just Words: Law, Language, and Power.* Chicago: University of Chicago Press.

Consedine, Jim. 2003. "The Maori Restorative Tradition." In *A Restorative Justice Reader* edited by Gerry Johnstone, pp. 152–157. Portland, OR: Willan Publishing.

David, Rene and John Brierly. 1985. *Major Legal Systems of the World Today.* London: Collier-Macmillan, Ltd.

Donovan, James and H. Edwin Anderson, III. 2003. *Anthropology & Law.* New York: Berghahn Books.

Erickson, Rosemary and Rita Simon. 1998. *The Use of Social Science Data in Supreme Court Decisions.* Urbana: University of Illinois Press.

Galanter, Marc. 1986. "When Legal Worlds Collide: Reflections on Bhopal, the Good Lawyer, and the American Law School." *Journal of Legal Education* 36:292–310.

Ghai, Yash, Robin Luckham and Francis Snyder, eds. 1987. *The Political Economy of Law: A Third World Reader.* New Delhi: Oxford University Press.

Glendon, Mary Ann, Michael Gordon and Paolo Carozza. 1999. *Comparative Legal Traditions.* St. Paul, MN: West Group.

Gluckman, Max. 1965. *The Ideas in Barotse Jurisprudence.* New Haven, CT: Yale University Press.

Goldman, Laurance. 1986. "A Case of 'Questions' and the Question of 'Case.'" *Text* 6:345–92.

Goldstein, Taryn, 1994. "Cultural Conflicts in Court: Should the American Criminal Justice System Formally Recognize a 'Cultural Defense'?" *Dickenson Law Review* 99:141–143.

Goodale, Mark. 2002. "Legal Ethnography in an Era of Globalization: The Arrival of Western Human Rights Discourse to Rural Bolivia." In *Practicing Ethnography in Law: New Dialogues, Enduring Methods,* edited by June Starr and Mark Goodale, pp. 50–71. New York: Palgrave, Macmillan.

Greenhouse, Carol, Barbara Yngvesson and David Engel. 1994. *Law and Community in Three American Towns.* Ithaca, NY: Cornell University Press.

Gulbrandsen, Ørnulf. 1996. "Living Their Lives in Courts: The Hegemonic Force of the Tswana Kgotla in a Colonial Context." In *Inside and Outside the Law: Anthropological Studies of Authority and Ambiguity*, edited by Olivia Harris, pp. 125–156. New York: Routledge.

Gulliver, P. H. 1969. "Dispute Settlement Without Courts: The Ndendeuli of Southern Tanzania." In *Law in Culture and Society*, edited by Laura Nader, pp. 24–68. Berkeley: University of California Press.

Hallaq, Wael. 1984 ""Was the Gate of Ijtihad Closed?" *International Journal of Middle East Studies* 16:3–41.

Harring, Sydney L. 1994. *Crow Dog's Case: American Indian Sovereignty, Tribal Law, and United States Law in the Nineteenth Century*. New York: Cambridge University Press.

Harris, Marvin. 1974. *Cows, Pigs, Wars & Witches*. New York: Random House, Inc.

Hawley, John. 1994. *Sati, the Blessing and the Course: The Burning of Wives in India*. New York: Oxford University Press.

Hayden, Robert. 1987. "Turn-Taking, Overlap, and the Task at Hand: Ordering Speaking Turns in Legal Settings." *American Ethnologist* 14:251–270.

Hirsch, Susan. 2002. "Feminist Participatory Research on Legal Consciousness." In *Practicing Ethnography in Law: New Dialogues, Enduring Methods*, edited by June Starr and Mark Goodale, pp. 13–33. New York: Palgrave, Macmillan.

Hoebel, E. Adamson. 1954. *The Law of Primitive Man: A Study in Comparative Legal Dynamics*. Cambridge: Harvard University Press.

Hostetler, John. 1993. *Amish Society*. Baltimore: Johns Hopkins Press.

Jewish Encyclopedia. 2002. Retrieved September 6, 2004. http://www.jewishencyclopedia.com./view.jsp?artid=939&letter=C&search=custom

Johnstone, Gerry. 2003. "Introduction: Restorative Approaches to Criminal Justice." In *A Restorative Justice Reader*, edited by Gerry Johnstone, pp. 1–18. Portland, OR: Willan Publishing.

Kidder, Robert and John Hostetler. 1990. 'Managing Ideologies: Harmony as an Ideology in Amish and Japanese Societies." *Law & Society Review* 24:895–922.

Kritzer, Herbert. 2002. "Stories from the Field: Collecting Data Outside Over There" In *Practicing Ethnography in Law: New Dialogues, Enduring Methods*, edited by June Starr and Mark Goodale, pp. 143–159. New York: Palgrave, Macmillan.

Lacey, Robert. 1998. *Sotheby's: Bidding for Class*. Boston: Little, Brown and Company.

Llewellyn, Karl and E. Adamson Hoebel. 1941. *The Cheyenne Way: Conflict and Case Law in Primitive Jurisprudence*. Norman: University of Oklahoma Press.

Lyman, John. 1986. "Cultural Defense: Viable Doctrine or Wishful Thinking?" *Criminal Justice Journal* 9: 87–117.

Mani, Lata. 1987. "Contentious Traditions: The Debate on Sati in Colonial India." *Cultural Critique* 7:119–156.

————. 1998. *Contentious Traditions: The Debate on Sati in Colonial India.* Berkeley: University of California Press.

Merry, Sally Engle. 1986. "Everyday Understanding of the Law in Working-Class America." *American Ethnologist* 13:253–270.

————. 1992. "Anthropology, Law, and Transnational Processes." *Annual Review of Anthropology* 21:357–79.

————. 2000. *Colonizing Hawaii.* Princeton, NJ: Princeton University Press.

Moore, Sally Falk. 1978. *Law as Process: An Anthropological Approach.* London: Routledge & Kegan Paul.

————. 2005. *Law and Anthropology: A Reader.* Malden, MA: Blackwell Publishing.

Morris, Virginia, Abdulkader Thomas and Yusuf Talal DeLorenzo. 2002. *Guide to Understanding Islamic Home Financing in Accordance with Islamic Shariah.* New York: Lightbulb Press.

Nader, Laura. 2002. *The Life of the Law.* Berkeley: University of California Press.

Nader, Laura and H. Todd, Jr, eds. 1978. *The Disputing Process—Law in Ten Societies.* New York: Columbia University Press.

Nasr, Seyyed Hossein. 2003. *Islam: Religion, History, and Civilization.* San Francisco: Harper-San Francisco.

Norgren, Jill and Serena Nanda. 1996. *American Cultural Pluralism and Law,* 2nd ed. Westport, CT: Praeger.

Oldenberg, Veena Talwar. 1994. "The Roop Kanwar Case: Feminist Responses" In *Sati, The Blessing and the Curse* edited by John Stratton Hawley, pp. 101–130. New York: Oxford University Press.

Orenstein, Henry. 1968. "The Ethnological Theories of Henry Sumner Maine." *American Anthropologist* 70:264–276.

Perry, Richard J. 1996. *From Time Immemorial: Indigenous People and State Systems.* Austin: University of Texas Press.

Pospisil, Leopold. 1978. *The Ethnology of Law,* 2nd ed. Menlo Park, CA: Cummings Publishing Company.

Quigley, John. 1989. "Socialist Law and the Civil Law Tradition." *The American Journal of Comparative Law* 37:781–808.

Radin, Max. 1938. "A Restatement of Hohfield." *Harvard Law Review* 51:1141–1164.

Reichel, Philip. 1999. *Comparative Criminal Justice Systems: A Topical Approach.* Upper Saddle River, NJ: Prentice Hall.

Renteln, Alison. 1993. "A Justification of the Cultural Defense as a Partial Excuse." *Review of Law and Women's Studies* 2:437–526.

————. 2004. *The Cultural Defense.* New York: Oxford University Press.

Reuters. 2003. *Desperate Indian Widows Sing Hymns for a Living.* Retrieved September 16, 2004 from http://www.vina.cc/stories/ GENERAL/2003/3/widowsinvrindavan.html.

Rich, Tracey. 2004. *Judaism 101.* Retrieved September 5, 2004. from http://www.jewfaq.org/halakhah.htm.

Rosen, Lawrence. 1977. "The Anthropologist as Expert Witness." *American Anthropologist* 79:555–578.

———. 1980. "Equity and Discretion in a Modern Islamic Legal System." *Law and Society Review* 15:217–18.

———. 1984. *Bargaining for Reality: The Construction of Social Relations in a Muslim Community.* Chicago: University of Chicago Press.

———. 1989. *The Anthropology of Justice: Law as Culture in Islamic Society.* Cambridge: Cambridge University Press.

Ross, Rupert. 2003. "Returning to the Teachings." In *A Restorative Justice Reader,* edited by Gerry Johnstone, pp. 125–143. Portland, OR: Willan Publishing.

Rouland, Norbert. 2005. "Criticism of Maine's Theory." In *Law and Anthropology: A Reader,* edited by Sally Falk Moore, pp. 22–23. Malden, MA: Blackwell Publishing.

Saks, Valerie. 1996. "An Indefensible Defense: On the Misuse of Culture in Criminal Law." *Arizona Journal of International & Comparative Law* 13:523–551.

Scheingold, Stuart. (1988) "Constitutional Rights and Social Change: Civil Rights in Perspective." In *Critical Perspectives on the Constitution,* edited by Michael W. McCann and Gerald L. Houseman. Boston: Little, Brown.

Seabrook, J. 2002. "In the City of Widows" *The Statesman* 13 October. Retrieved 15 September 2004 http://bridget.jatol.com/pipermail/sacw_net/2002/001640.htm

Simpson, Lesley. 1966. *The Encomienda of New Spain (rev. ed).* Berkeley: University of California Press.

Starr, June and Jane F. Collier. 1989. *History and Power in the Study of Law: New Directions in Legal Anthropology.* Ithaca: Cornell University Press.

Starr, June and Mark Goodale, eds. 2002. *Practicing Ethnography in Law.* New York: Palgrave, Macmillan.

Van Cott, Donna. 2003. "Legal Pluralism and Informal Community Justice in Latin America." Paper prepared for the conference Informal Institutions and Latin American Politics, April 24–25.

Vold, George B. 1958. *Theoretical Criminology.* New York: Oxford University Press.

Volpp, Leti. 1994. "(Mis)Identifying Culture: Asian Women and the "Cultural Defense.'" *Harvard Women's Law Journal* 17:57.

Watson, Alan. 1981. *The Making of the Civil Law.* 1981. Cambridge: Harvard University Press.

Wu, Michele Wen Chen. 2003. "Comment: Culture Is No Defense for Infanticide." *American University Journal of Gender, Social Policy & Law* 11:975–1022.

Yerbury, J. Colin and Curt Griffiths. 1999. "Minorities, Crime, and the Law." In *Diversity Justice in Canada,* edited by John Winterdyk and Douglas King, pp. 26–34. Toronto: Canadian Scholars Press, Inc.

Yngvesson, Barbara. 1990. "Contextualizing the Courts: Comments on the Cultural Study of Litigation." *Law & Society Review* 24:467–476.

Index